Parker

Rockmount

LEGENDS

◆LEGENDS◆

CELEBRITIES IN CLASSIC AMERICAN FASHION

STEVE WEIL

Gibbs Smith

First Edition
30 29 28 27 26 5 4 3 2 1

Photograph credits: page 183

Published by
Gibbs Smith
570 N. Sportsplex Drive
Kaysville, Utah 84037
www.gibbs-smith.com

The authorized representative in the EEA is Simon and Schuster Netherlands BV, Herculesplein 96 3584 AA Utrecht, Netherlands, info@simonandschuster.nl

Designed by Sheryl Dickert
Printed and bound in China

Library of Congress Control Number: 2025945319
ISBN: 978-1-4236-6953-1
This product is made of FSC®-certified and other controlled material.

Contents

RRW
Rockmount
Ranch Wear
DENVER COLO.
Since 1946
Styled in the West by Westerners

Preface

My first book, *Western Shirts: A Classic American Fashion* (coauthored with G. DeWeese) was published by Gibbs Smith in 2004. After the first book, I wrote another one to document my grandfather's amazing life, accomplishments, and personality—*Ask Papa Jack: Wisdom of the World's Oldest CEO.*

Running a viable business pays the bills, but Rockmount Ranch Wear Mfg. Co. is more than that: it has been my family's lifework. This inspired me to begin an archival collection, not as a mere hobby, but to document and preserve fashion history—the actual shirts, hats and accessories, memorabilia, advertising, signage, and more—that traces the history of a special area of Americana. I started collecting *vintage* Rockmount before that term was in use. I found my first shirt while in high school, working part-time in our 1909 brick and timbered Wazee Street warehouse. I found an ancient women's two-tone embroidered shirt stuffed and lost in a shelving crevice on the fifth floor; somehow it survived decades, for me to find in the mid-1970s. It was a factory second and was never sold. I sensed the intrinsic importance of things like this and documented them along with recollections of my father and grandfather, who worked together for fifty years.

Later, in the 1980s, I read *Cadillac Jack* by Larry McMurtry (whom I had the pleasure of meeting many years later; but that is another story for later in the book). It was somewhat autobiographical, about a guy who traveled the country in an old Cadillac unearthing Ming vases and other special finds, including old cowboy boots at flea markets, estate sales, and so on. The plot includes a bookstore and gallery in Washington, DC (which Larry actually had), where he displayed the boots. The important point is that vintage clothing was not yet a concept. Sure, there were used clothing stores, but it had not become a thing. Years later, collecting vintage became popular here and in Japan and Europe, and an industry emerged.

So, back in the '80s I began displaying our historical memorabilia and shirts on the walls at Rockmount. Some of the shirts I had absconded with from my grandfather's closet. He continued wearing shirts he made in the '40s and '50s fifty years later. It presented a dilemma to me because they were museum pieces; but he had made them, so who better to keep wearing them all these decades later. I thought they should be preserved and put on display, and they were, until I noticed nails in the wall with nothing there because he'd taken them home to wear! Over the ensuing years, I scoured used clothing shops in Denver and every place I traveled across the country, Europe, and Japan. Other like-minded people sent me special ones to preserve in our archive. Museums and collectors let me study their collections.

Reading Larry McMurtry helped me realize I was on the right path, and thus began the Rockmount archive, later exhibited at many museums, including the Autry (Los Angeles), Buffalo Bill Center of the West (an affiliate of the Smithsonian, Cody, Wyoming), Denver Art Museum, History Colorado Museum, Foothills Museum (Golden, Colorado), National Cowboy & Western Heritage Center in several exhibits (Oklahoma City), and even in the Smithsonian, the nation's ultimate museum.

My grandfather was a no-nonsense guy who made stuff, sold it, and then repeated the process for eighty years. He was not the sentimental type. Dad, on the other hand, was an artist in the true sense of the word. He instilled in me an eye and love of good design and museums. His abstract art was shown in the Denver Art Museum in the '60s. He took me on my first trip to New York City, where we hit the usual suspects. That inspired me to visit museums on all my travels across the US, Europe, Asia. Later, I met curators at the Buffalo Bill Center of the West, and when a design conference was scheduled at the museum, I was invited to participate, a relationship that is going on thirty years now.

The labor of love to write the first book began in 2003 when I met Gibbs Smith, the prolific publisher, in Cody. We were attending the Western Design Conference and had a fascinating conversation over lunch at Buffalo Bill's Irma Hotel. Gibbs told me I should write a book, and he would publish it. Skeptical, I said, "Yeah, I should be a rock star too!" But he was serious and shepherded me through the process. We became friends. He was a true renaissance man from Utah. We both had vintage Airstream trailers, but he actually traveled in his (abhorred airplanes), whereas mine was parked in a camping spot in the mountains. I spent enough time with Gibbs and Cathy Smith to grasp that they appreciated a world filled with diverse views. We met many times. My fondest memories are when he took me to a Leonard Cohen concert at Red Rocks, and I became a devotee of Cohen's soulful music.

The Gibbs Smith publishing catalog had works in the thousands covering diverse subjects from popular culture to education, architecture, and more. Gibbs understood the Western ethos. He is gone, and Cathy has retired from the business, but the company continues on under an ESOP owned by the employees.

I had been asking myself for a long time if I had a third book in me. So, when, in August 2024, an unexpected call came from editor Madge Baird saying her team was enthusiastic about a new edition, it didn't take more than a few minutes for me to say yes, I have a third book in me! What emerged from our discussions was a new direction based on Rockmount's amazing celebrity following. Although Rockmount's popularity on screen and stage goes back decades, it has surfaced more clearly since the earlier books. Having the publisher's support, editorial, graphics, and marketing allowed me to stick to running my business and writing as time permitted.

As we formed a publication schedule, I realized the release date in 2026 would be Rockmount's 80th anniversary! Perfect! What better way to celebrate the role this family firm has had in fashion and mainstream culture than a new book? *Rockmount Legends* is a memoir of my family's three-generation legacy in helping create a true American fashion. While we are a small business, Rockmount Ranch Wear has an integral role beyond the Western apparel industry and has impacted world fashion. The business has supported hundreds of people, even thousands when you consider its administration, factories, suppliers, and sales throughout the US and most developed countries.

A lot has happened in twenty years. My father and grandfather are gone, yet their presence is strong. Papa's obituary ran in the *Economist, New York Times,* and over 200 papers around the world. The company built on their foundation thrives. Our music and screen presence has exploded. The stories burgeoned; some made news media, but, of course, print is not what it used to be. While we have a strong online presence, these remarkable stories deserve to be in print. Many came from my weekly essay in our newsletter.

The internet is the biggest existential change in the past two decades, maybe world history. It has the potential to unify us if we don't let it polarize us. It gave this small family company on Denver's Wazee Street the reach to all corners of the planet. In the past, only big companies had the resources to reach the world, but now, any size company can. Our reach extends from Tokyo to Los Angeles, Marfa and Santa Fe, Paris, and even Antarctica. This is a memoir of our continuing work to make the world safe for Western wear. Evolve or die in obscurity—as Papa instilled—innovate, innovate!

I hope you enjoy reading this book as much as I enjoyed writing it. Here's to the next 80 years!

ASK PAPA JACK

An American Original and True Entrepreneur

Jack A. Weil was all about innovation from the day he opened Rockmount's doors in 1946 to the day he left in 2008, at age 107. He followed his own path, not looking at others for inspiration—something he instilled in my father and me. He shares this trait with the ubiquitous entrepreneurs of our day, who each brought something new to market.

Papa Jack used to say he "never wanted to be the richest guy in the cemetery." He exuded a kind of warmth and compassion too seldom seen in big business. His family was always smitten by his wry sense of humor, wit, common sense, and sage advice. His driving, not so much. The industry knew him, but not the public at large. That came with the press in the later years and also by our opening a flagship retail store on Wazee in what was our 1909 warehouse; it became a historic landmark. The mayor named the street in his honor upon his 100th birthday, updating it every year until his 107th.

RIGHT: At 17th and Wazee Street in Denver. Humboldt is head of security.

ENTREPRENEURIAL CHARACTER

Entrepreneurs share certain traits. While Rockmount remains a small company, it is rooted in some of the same characteristics seen in other innovators. Papa Jack was a highly unusual personality who made seismic design changes in his field. It started with his exciting idea to design and make Western clothing to help give Westerners their own special identity, then the ability to manufacture it, bring it to market, and, finally, to create a lasting brand.

Papa Jack was not a conventional thinker, and this enabled his new idea of creating a fashion for Westerners to grow and flourish. This counterintuitive thinking was present in his business philosophy. He eschewed the big chains and instead committed his support to independent retailers, who built the middle class. He took pride in refusing to sell to the big-box category killers. Today, we maintain this position and relegate mega-size online retailers (who have decimated small, locally owned retail) to the no-go category.

He ran his business conservatively, retaining earnings in the company to avoid borrowing from banks, which can

Rockmount Wholesale Catalog, 1940s.
ABOVE: Jack A's son, Jack B, modeling hat in top right corner, daughter Jane is the model below him.

Mr. & Mrs. Home-town INDEPENDENT MERCHANT—
When You Buy ROCKMOUNT RANCH WEAR, YOU BUY Newest Authentic Styling, Complete Selections, American Materials, Right Prices, At Once Deliveries. YOU BUY Shirts, Pants, Hats, Belts and Buckles, Ties, Collar Points all from THE ONE FIRM for INDEPENDENT MERCHANTS.
RRW
Rockmount Ranch Wear
DENVER COLO
ORIGINAL WASHABLE MODEL
100 FAST-SELLING STYLES WRITE FOR OUR SALESMAN TO CALL, or We'll Send Samples
COMPANION STALLIONS
DRIP-DRY BROADCLOTH STRIKING EMBROIDERED COMBINATIONS
To Sell Profitably from $3.95 to $5.95
Solid Color & Patterned Short Sleeve Models

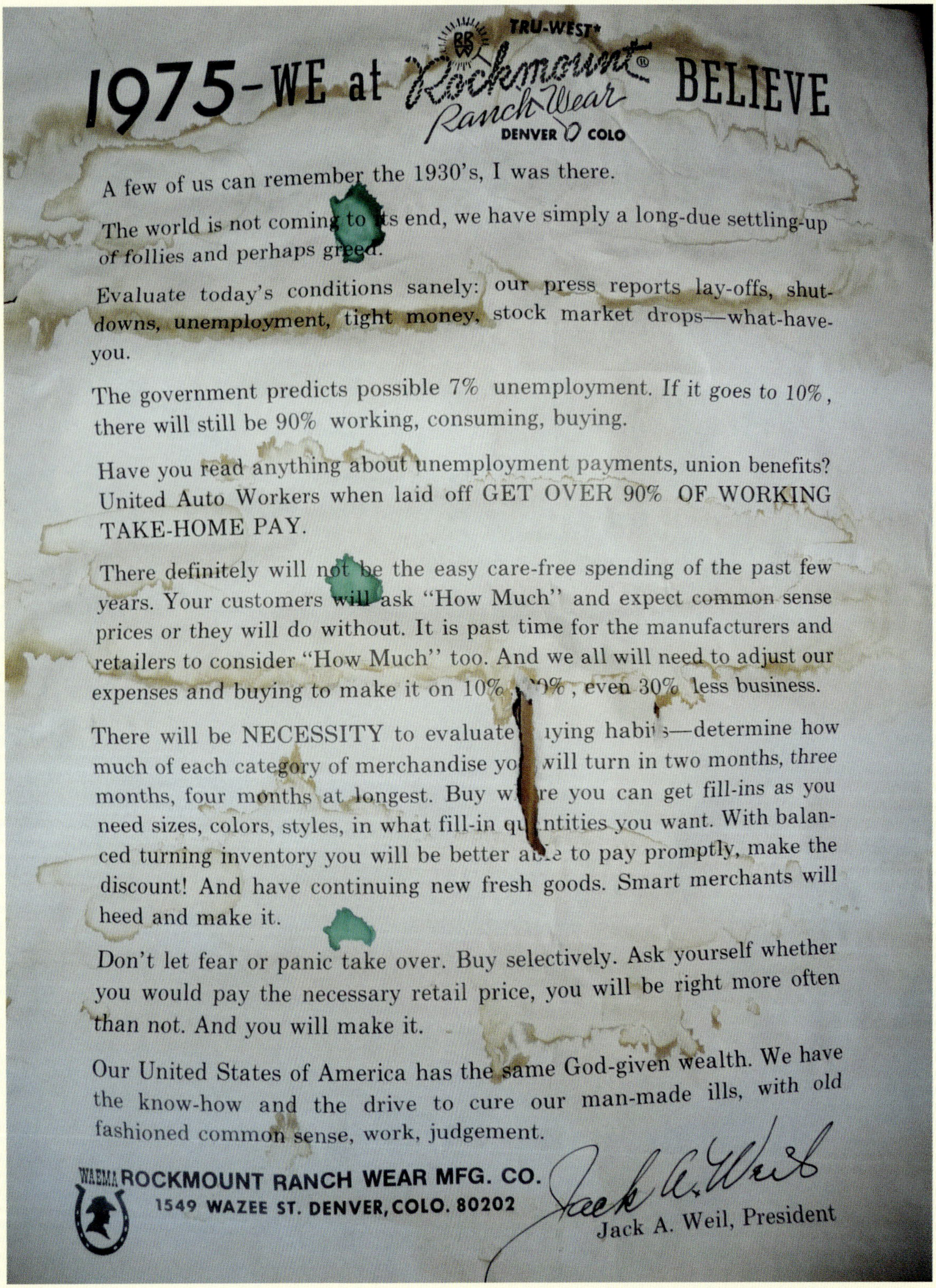

TRU-WEST®

1975-WE at Rockmount® Ranch Wear DENVER COLO BELIEVE

A few of us can remember the 1930's, I was there.

The world is not coming to its end, we have simply a long-due settling-up of follies and perhaps greed.

Evaluate today's conditions sanely: our press reports lay-offs, shut-downs, unemployment, tight money, stock market drops—what-have-you.

The government predicts possible 7% unemployment. If it goes to 10%, there will still be 90% working, consuming, buying.

Have you read anything about unemployment payments, union benefits? United Auto Workers when laid off GET OVER 90% OF WORKING TAKE-HOME PAY.

There definitely will not be the easy care-free spending of the past few years. Your customers will ask "How Much" and expect common sense prices or they will do without. It is past time for the manufacturers and retailers to consider "How Much" too. And we all will need to adjust our expenses and buying to make it on 10%, 20%, even 30% less business.

There will be NECESSITY to evaluate buying habits—determine how much of each category of merchandise you will turn in two months, three months, four months at longest. Buy where you can get fill-ins as you need sizes, colors, styles, in what fill-in quantities you want. With balanced turning inventory you will be better able to pay promptly, make the discount! And have continuing new fresh goods. Smart merchants will heed and make it.

Don't let fear or panic take over. Buy selectively. Ask yourself whether you would pay the necessary retail price, you will be right more often than not. And you will make it.

Our United States of America has the same God-given wealth. We have the know-how and the drive to cure our man-made ills, with old fashioned common sense, work, judgement.

WAEMA ROCKMOUNT RANCH WEAR MFG. CO.
1549 WAZEE ST. DENVER, COLO. 80202

Jack A. Weil

Jack A. Weil, President

ruin borrowers when economic conditions reverse. Papa Jack learned this lesson as a survivor of the Great Depression. Recessions typically occur in ten-year cycles; he survived a hundred years' worth.

Papa's philosophy helped me navigate the COVID-19 pandemic. I was vice president of the Denver Athletic Club at the time and had to decide if we should continue plans to do a $2 million renovation of the club, founded in 1884. There had been a bad recession in 1975, and Papa printed a poster to show our customers at trade shows. His point was that during downturns it is important to invest in your business so that you are ready when things turn around, which they always do. My decision was made based on the advice in this poster.

It warms my heart to come across special things my family did since the company's inception eighty years ago. This ad sums up Papa Jack's philosophy and holds true today, three generations later. Most family businesses have integrity, lacking so much today in big businesses that are based on algorithms lacking human spirit, personal contact, scale, and presence. Resistance is not futile—while *Star Trek*'s Borg has infiltrated much of modern life, it is, fortunately, not everywhere.

We continue the good fight of producing all we can in the USA. We pay a living wage, have never had a layoff, and have employed thousands over the past eight decades. We also create what we do on our own terms, not by shopping the market and knocking off others' better ideas, which is common in the fashion industry.

THE POWER OF PERSONAL CONTACT

Personal contact is one of the central tenets of humanity. AI can, of course, be one solution to the challenges facing mankind but at great risk of existential detriment. While Papa Jack was an early adopter of the computer in the sixties, he thought of it as an efficient tool, not as a replacement for decision-making based on ethical behavior. New-school entrepreneurs seem to be all about algorithms and digital computer processes—inhuman at worst and non-human at best. This is lost in a world without actual human contact and support. Some businesses understand that better than others, but they tend to be locally owned and run.

Papa Jack never met a person he didn't like (channeling Will Rogers). He met thousands of people every year and yet remembered the names of their kids and even their dogs. When someone told him where they lived, he knew something about the place, wherever it was, especially the small towns.

OPPOSITE: Jack A's letter to retailers on how to overcome a bad recession.

RIGHT: Rockmount wholesale ad, 1950s.

PROFILE—Three Generations

The Rockmount Ranch Wear Manufacturing Co. of Denver was founded twelve years ago by Jack A. Weil who has been associated with the Western Wear business since the early 1930's. His son, Jack B. Weil, now 30, entered the business after his discharge from the army in 1954.

The elder Mr. Weil is a pioneer in the Western Wear field, and has seen many of the innovations of past years now fully accepted. With others he is responsible for the present universal use of the pearl snap button on western shirts, and introduced into the industry the idea of tailored Western Wear for general sports wear, styling the shirts away from the early standard satin-piped, denim, and plain gabardine, which were largely the only factory-made shirts of the day.

One of the original ideas was the matching ladies' and men's shirts for general wear with the ladies' shirts having styled collars for casual or "rodeo" wear, and many of the basic patterns in use today for the Western shirt were originally cut by Mr. Weil.

He is recognized as a leader in the field with constantly new yoke styles and fabrics coming out of the Rockmount factories with currently over 100 shirt styles representing several thousands of dozens of shirts in stock for "same day" shipment.

The company on its formation set several sales policies from which it has never varied. All merchandise, which includes a complete line of wool-felt hats, straws, buckles, belts, ties, accessories, as well as shirts carry the one label ROCKMOUNT. The business is entirely wholesale with no retail sales, nor any direct-to-consumer affiliates, with sales to independent merchants only.

Rockmount Ranch Wear is a large but personalized business with either father or son always available to talk business or just visit with anyone who comes in to the downtown Denver business office. Both take part in civic affairs. Jack Jr. is a part of the welcoming committee of the Colorado Centennial celebration, and Jack Sr. this year is Chairman of the Colorado Apparel Manufacturers of the Colorado Centennial Commission, and is also vice-president of the Market Development Committee of the Denver Chamber of Commerce.

Between the two Jacks, they are personal friends of the majority of their customers, and while the total number of customers is imposing, and still growing, their ambition is to be personally acquainted with all of them. With third generation Steven already making his share of friends they may well get it done.

Third generation Steven with his grandfather Jack A. Weil, and be-whiskered dad Jack B. Weil; the beard is temporary in honor of Colorado's Centennial. Young Steven, 18 months, is already a model and "showpiece" in his western outfit. This picture was taken in the sample room of the Rockmount Ranch Wear business office at 1636 Lawrence St. in Denver, Colorado.

Western Wear & Equipment, trade magazine profile of three generations of Weils, 1959.

INDIVIDUALISM IS AT THE CORE

Why is Papa Jack's vision of Western fashion and individuality still running strong all these decades later? Why does it have enduring appeal that has permeated screen, stage, and lifestyle? At its root, it's the ongoing appeal of Americana, both in the US and abroad. In the late nineteenth century, Buffalo Bill took the West around the world, popularizing the public's love of the American West. People love the concept of individualism represented by Native American and cowboy cultures unique to the American West. Papa Jack perceived that during the Great Depression, and he began the first company dedicated to Western clothing. While other companies made some Western clothing, they weren't 100 percent Western, as is Rockmount.

A fundamental tenet of individualism is that it is tied to capitalism in the free world. Old-school entrepreneurs reveled in the freedom of the individual and its potential to create. Individualism is perhaps the root of the fundamental attraction of Western shirts in particular and Western culture overall. Not to oversimplify, but the world's opposing forces seem to be the struggle of individual freedom versus totalitarianism at worst and the tyranny of convention at best. In its small way, Western fashion emanates from the cultures that celebrate freedom and individual choice. Why else did protest movements of the 1960s often see so many Western shirts on concert stages, film, and their audiences? This has helped lead to its enduring place in the world.

ROCKMOUNT OPENS RETAIL

We never sold retail until 2001, because Papa and Dad did not want to step on the toes of local retailers who carried Rockmount. One day in 2001, we were eating lunch across the street at the Oxford Hotel. We watched an endless stream of people walk in Rockmount's doors despite signs on both sides saying "Wholesale Only." The retail landscape had fundamentally changed, and the main street stores had disappeared (not just in Denver but across the country and beyond). The closest store was ten miles away. So, I made a case to Papa and Dad for opening retail, and they agreed. Innovation was central to the launch of our business, and this later pivot surreptitiously became a key ingredient giving us a future in an environment increasingly overwhelmed by business consolidation.

The original store was my dad's repurposed private office, which he was using more like a closet—about 15 x 15 feet with gridwall panels for hanging shirts. It was a strange setup, but people loved coming into our historic building, office, and warehouse, as it was unlike anything they had ever seen. It proved a success, so when Dad and I bought the building from the family, we decided to undertake a major restoration. The joke was, we remodel every fifty years whether we need to or not.

During this time, we had been invited to open our first retail store in a new mall built by Colorado Mills with no financial risk. They built it out for us. We learned how to do retail, after more than fifty years of wholesale only.

Papa was 106 years old and instantly took on the role of chief greeter. At an industry party we hosted, Papa was asked by a journalist, "Who are the big shots?" True to form, he responded, "The big shots get enough media attention. Let me introduce you to the small shots."

He came from the Midwest and never lost his roots. Our flagship store on Wazee Street turned out to be a great move. While we had had closeouts in the wholesale-only era due to key sizes selling out (stores only wanted complete size runs), leaving the residual, we never put anything on sale in our retail store because everything sold out, to the piece. Also very important to Rockmount's brand integrity, we built this next stage of business growth to be based on special design and quality, not price. The best thing, however, was that we finally had direct contact with the consumer, something missing the prior fifty years. We simply shifted our wholesale culture of closer customer relationships to retail, and it has been expanding yearly since 2001.

So, Rockmount, founded by Papa Jack, celebrates its 80th anniversary in 2026. Papa worked until age 107 with passion and never took his eye off the ball. He originated snap shirts worn across the world. He supported small, independent retailers by not discounting to majors. He gave credit with a handshake. Many of the retailers he did business with thrive today, after decades of carrying Rockmount, such as Taubert's in Casper, Wyoming, founded in 1919; Wall Drug in South Dakota, which goes back to the Great Depression; Scott Colburn in Livonia, Michigan, from the 1950s; F.M. Light in Steamboat Springs, founded in 1905.

COMPASSION IN BUSINESS

We heard from an old retailer how Rockmount helped them stay in business. Supporting independent retailers is in our DNA, which is more important now than ever. The ski-area retailer ran into trouble during a no-snow year. Turns out, Papa Jack helped him, as he did many stores around the country. This is not an isolated case but an ingrained part of our ethos at Rockmount, and it's nice when someone takes the time to let us know.

Papa Jack started Rockmount and made the first snap Western shirts, but he was more than an entrepreneur. Small family businesses bring more to the table than widgets and numbers. They form a vital part of our economy and society, and it's good to be reminded of it. Integrity is rooted in the West and its unique way of life. This is the stuff they don't teach you in business school. We hope you enjoy it, too.

This email came to Rockmount Aug. 17, 2018, from Charlie Davis:

> *Always on my mind—what an incredible man Jack Weil was and [he] was such an inspiration to me. He saved my store, Wild West, Steamboat Springs, in the year the Ski Corp closed our winter season, as a result of that no snow year.*
>
> *Recently, traveling in New Mexico, Abiquiu Inn and gift shop, I had the privilege of seeing Jack's Rockmount shirts on prominent display.*
>
> *He lives on with the best of memories.*
>
> *My best of regards,*
>
> *Charlie Davis*

Steve Weil replied Aug. 18:

Charlie,

Thanks for taking the time to write. My grandfather had a good heart, something that seems lost in today's global economy. His integrity inspires us and we do our best to live up to it.

Regards,

Steve Weil, President & Chief Creative Officer

Then Charlie replied with the whole story, which just keeps getting better.

In a message dated August 18:

This is a copy of an email sent to my daughter and son, thought you might like to see.

Remember the year of the snow drought in Steamboat? I had just opened a new Wild West in Jackson Hole and filled Wild West Steamboat and Wild West Jackson Hole with merchandise for peak season . . . and owed a ton of accounts payable. LTV closed the ski mountain early and did not open until late March.

Jane Romberg's father, Jack Weil, president and owner of one of my major vendors, Rockmount Ranch Wear, called me that day. He said, "Charlie, Jane told me they closed the mountain today. That will bring on a rash of 'pushy corporate types' demanding money. Have an answer for them in the form of a plan to repay them. As for Rockmount Ranch Wear, forget paying me until the next season comes and makes you whole. It will always snow in Colorado and Western wear will not go out of style. Next year will be good to you." Jack Weil was the first vendor I repaid.

He lived to be over 100. He was famous for inventing the snap western wear shirt and was interviewed on national TV 60 Minutes. What I remember most about Jack was his integrity and moral nature. He told me there is more on an invoice than 40 days net 20.

Jack Weil once told me of a dear friend that died and named him as executor of this estate. After the estate was settled, the attorney and bank trust officers asked for his bill. He could have collected $10,000 plus expenses. He responded, "This was my friend and he would not have charged me a cent. Therefore, you will see no bill from me."

Jack was an inspiration and I had always wanted to follow his lead. I had a close friend client when I was a financial advisor that had the confidence in me to place a considerable sum of money to invest and fortunately his portfolio profit grew to better than a million dollars. He passed away and his executor, a federal judge and son in law asked me to liquidate the account. I responded, "There will be no fees, commissions and expenses." He looked at me as if I was crazy and wanted to know why I was walking away from thousands of dollars in legitimate commissions. My response was, "You can thank Jack Weil." Joe, my client, was a close friend. I worked on a fee base and we both made money. He of course did not know Jack.

Soon after that I joined the Peace Corps in response of the 9/11 tragedy. I was in a training class in Romania. The instructor asked for names of people in their lives that made a difference. The class responded with Winston Churchill, Franklin Roosevelt, John Kennedy, and many others.

My response, JACK WEIL.

Charlie Davis

When re-reading this, it gives me chills. We knew our grandfather and family patriarch was special, but when others share these stories, it validates what we felt.

ROCKMOUNT.
THREE GENERATIONS OF CLASSIC AMERICAN FASHION.
DESIGNED IN THE AMERICAN WEST • MADE IN THE USA

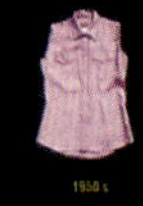

THE ROCKMOUNT STORY

Rockmount Ranch Wear Mfg. Co. is the oldest Western snap shirt manufacturer, and my grandfather Jack A. Weil (1901-2008), the founder, is considered the originator of Western shirts. Papa Jack's innovations in the design and production of Western shirts helped launch an industry and define a lifestyle.

His lifelong career in apparel began at D.S. Bernstein Overall Factory in Evansville, Indiana, while in high school in 1918 during WWI. What he learned there on the factory floor as a teenager directly impacted his future career and the direction of Western fashion.

Jack A. moved to Denver, Colorado, in 1928 with his young wife, Bea. An early adopter of innovation, he drove one of the first Chryslers, a 1926 roadster, across the Great Plains to Colorado. In Denver, he opened a sales office for A. Stein & Co., a Chicago-based company that manufactured elastic webbing products, including garters, suspenders, and rubber sundries. The company was founded in 1887, and its most popular brand was Paris Garters.

In 1933, he went into business with his friend Phil Miller, of Miller & Co., the earliest exclusively Western wear manufacturer. Together they built a company that prospered despite, and perhaps because of, the Great Depression.

OPPOSITE: This poster, based on a painting of the three generations, which I commissioned from David Parker, was sent to over a thousand Rockmount retailers to display in their stores in the early 1990s.

ABOVE: Denver, 1934, 16th & Curtis, where Jack A. opened his office for Paris Garters, on the left side of the street.

At Miller, Jack developed a new style of shirt for their farm and ranch customers that came to be known as Western wear. An American phenomenon, Western wear gained popularity first by creating a fashion identity for Westerners to distinguish themselves from the conventional fashions worn everywhere else. People could escape the malaise of the Depression by identifying with real cowboys, as well as the mythic ones on the big screen. Jack and Phil hit a gold vein. They found a rural market—ranchers and farmers—that could afford Western clothing despite the worst economic conditions in modern history. The countercultural element of Western fashion extended to the industry itself, which would thrive during later recessions. (Interestingly, the Western industry, originally rural, was somewhat insulated from downturns that affected urban areas more, but that seems to have changed as its popularity became more widespread since the 1990s.) Wearing Western fashion simply made people happy in an otherwise dark time. Together, Phil and Jack launched a new look, America's only truly original fashion: Western wear.

Jack's responsibilities included design, manufacturing, and advertising. He loved to design and produce ornate, high-quality shirts. Jack also managed the retail catalog. He never liked working with the retail chains, which demanded price concessions at the expense of good design and quality construction. He felt Miller wanted him to compromise his values, so he left shortly after World War II ended, to found Rockmount Ranch Wear Mfg. Co.

Design and quality were core values for the rest of his career. His target market then was better specialty stores—just as it is today—not the discounters. His original commitment to small, locally owned businesses remains central to Rockmount's philosophy.

Jack originated many elements of classic Western shirt design, including the fit, front yokes, "sawtooth" pockets, and various fancy cuff treatments. His designs became fashion standards. Yokes accentuate a man's broad shoulders. Flap pockets secured their contents. Snaps were a "breakaway" feature so the shirt would not get caught on a saddle, branch, or steer horn. Long tails helped the shirt stay tucked in while riding horseback. Most importantly, the look was meant to be distinct from conventional boxy shirts of the era. Cowboys, ranchers, and Westerners wanted to be different from city slickers. In the tradition of the rugged individualism key to the cowboy ethos, Western clothing helped them define their special identity.

Much as Apple's Steve Jobs brought his product to the public by making products based on good design and innovation, Jack developed ways to make highly ornate Western clothes at affordable prices. At the same time, celebrities had custom-made shirts that cost several times that of Rockmount's similar designs. It's one thing to design nice shirts, but it's something entirely different—and complicated—to engineer their efficient production. Papa Jack was the driving force that made it happen.

The early big chains like Montgomery Ward, JCPenney, and Sears demanded cheaper goods. Rather than be dependent on these chain stores, Jack built Rockmount's distribution through independent retailers across the country. He felt a healthy economy depended on small-scale, grassroots businesses that employed American labor. This also enabled him to avoid compromising quality and design.

Stockman-Farmer retail catalog, 1940. Jack A. managed the merchandising and layout. Note 2 percent sales tax.

Whereas other manufacturers routinely discounted their prices to the large retail chains and charged higher prices to the smaller independent stores, Jack maintained a one-price label. His "one price" policy supported small retailers. His thinking: why should the little guy pay more, in effect subsidizing the discounters? Jack felt he could sell to a hundred independent stores the same amount as he could sell to a hundred-store chain, and he extended credit the old-fashioned way—with a handshake. Today, locally owned stores are badly hurt and unfairly challenged by internet retailers and big-box chains making the situation far worse for the consumer as retail consolidates. Papa Jack used to say, "Not all progress is improvement." Indeed, today, the trade-off for cheaper prices in the consolidation of retail leaves consumers with fewer choices and little or no customer service. Beyond that, Jack instilled Rockmount with the belief that discounting is detrimental to the middle class, which was built on mom-and-pop businesses across all sectors of the economy that have been—those that survive—hugely impacted and weakened.

Jack is known for being the first manufacturer to use snaps in shirts. To acknowledge that, I coined our longtime slogan "We Put the Snap in Western Shirts." His snap shirt design idea predated World War II but did not go into production until the war ended and manufacturing returned to a peacetime economy, when metal became more readily available again and could be used for snaps.

When Jack first approached a supplier for snaps to go on shirts, the company declined because it was a "misapplication." They eventually acquiesced after he got the management's attention by saying loudly in their New York office, "If I want to eat them as Post Toasties, that is my business." In fact, this design element, originated by Rockmount, became ubiquitous over many years.

People often ask if we patented the use of snaps. In fact, Papa Jack visited a New York City patent attorney to explore if it was feasible and left with the view that it was unenforceable. More importantly is that one company would never have popularized it to the extent possible with many brands that followed later.

Ad designed by Steve, early 1980s.

THE SECOND GENERATION JOINS THE BUSINESS

The process of building a market beyond the West surged in the mid-1950s when Jack A.'s son, Jack B. (1928–2008), joined the company in 1954. He began in sales and went on the road opening up independent retailers across the country. He was one of the first Western wear salesmen to introduce Western fashion to Americans east of the Mississippi.

Jack B. eventually took over Rockmount's design and merchandising roles, heading both for more than forty years. He also became the sales manager and continued in that role throughout his career. Because Jack A. had handled design for many years, it took him a long time to become comfortable with someone else doing it. It typified a universal and timeless generation gap. My dad told me that he created designs in his head for many years before his father let him do his own collection. Dad eventually became the driving force for merchandising all of Rockmount's collections, including apparel, hats, buckles, belts, bolo ties, and jewelry. During the 1960s, he became an abstract painter and a collector of modern art. This influenced Rockmount's designs; he was extremely creative and had a great eye and a broad aesthetic appreciation. As Rockmount was never about producing "just anything," our brand had to be special and distinctive, not more of the same as other brands.

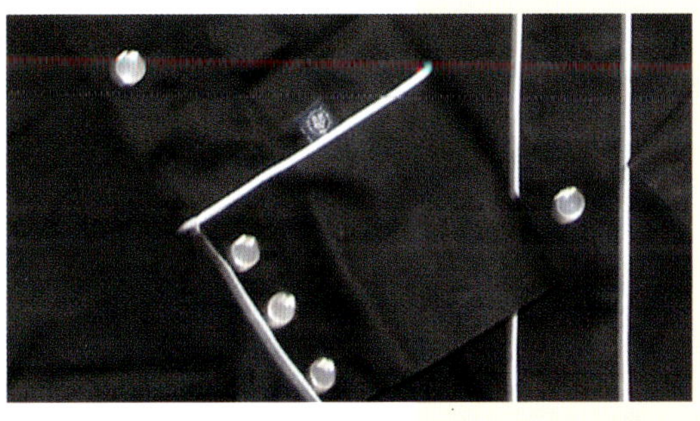

Jack B.'s innovations included the concept of matching shirts for men, women, and children. His navy cuff tag Rockmount Tru-West was trademarked in 1985. (At that time, Levi Strauss held the one and only other label-positioning trademark.) Jack B.'s lifeblood was creativity. He lived and breathed new designs of shirts, hats, and accessories, trying a constant stream of new and daring things. By doing this, he introduced styles that further helped popularize Western wear nationwide and resulted in early exports to Canada, Europe, Asia, and Australia.

Int. Cl.: 25

Prior U.S. Cl.: 39

Reg. No. 1,365,667

United States Patent and Trademark Office Registered Oct. 15, 1985

TRADEMARK
PRINCIPAL REGISTER

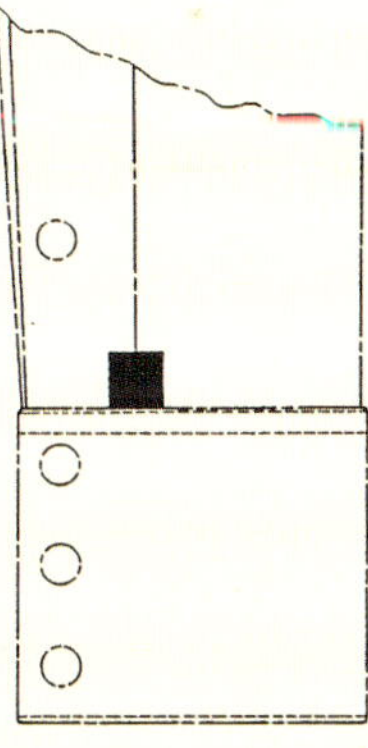

ROCKMOUNT RANCH WEAR MANUFACTURING COMPANY (COLORADO CORPORATION)
1626 WAZEE ST.
DENVER, CO 80202

FOR: SHIRTS FOR MEN, WOMEN, AND CHILDREN, IN CLASS 25 (U.S. CL. 39).
FIRST USE 1-1-1976; IN COMMERCE 1-1-1976.

THE MARK CONSISTS OF A RECTANGULAR TAB DEVICE SEWN ON THE CUFF OF A SHIRT AT A LOCATION APPROXIMATELY 2.5 CM FROM FROM THE SLEEVE POCKET.

SEC. 2(F).

SER. NO. 423,765, FILED 4-29-1983.

CRAIG K. MORRIS, EXAMINING ATTORNEY

THE THIRD GENERATION COMES ONBOARD

As the third generation of the family, I grew up in the business. During high school, I worked in the warehouse, sweeping the floors and packing boxes. I joined the company full time in 1981 and started in advertising and marketing, later working my way up through the company. In the mid-1980s, I went into design, creating shirt designs that my friends would wear. But I was always building on the foundation laid by my grandfather and father. In the late 1980s, we were approached by a major Japanese trading company to introduce Rockmount shirts to Japan. We had worked with the Disney theme parks, but this company eclipsed all of them and wanted authentic, high-quality American fashion with a story.

I worked with them to develop a collection aimed at young men; it became a sensation in Japan and remains popular today, which is a rarity there, where most trends are short-lived. These top-quality shirts ranged from denim, solids, plaids, and quirky prints—always with a twist. The Japanese preference for quality and design not dictated by price fit well with Rockmount. Their appreciation of Americana and classic looks influenced my design direction, which eventually took over our entire line by the mid-1990s.

Remaining true to our Western roots has taken Western wear to a new level of classic American fashion. This helps us avoid being pigeon-holed. We

do not follow mere trends that last but a season. Our goal is to create classic designs for the long term, and that also pertains to sustainability. Unlike fast fashion, which has a shorter wearable life, we believe our longer lasting designs and materials won't end up in landfills. Many of our customers tell us their favorite shirt is a Rockmount, ten or even fifteen years old.

In 1988, we introduced relaxed-fit shirts, an alternative to slim fit and now an industry standard. Our Rockmount vintage collection, one of my first design initiatives, began in the 1990s, long before any other company in the Western industry did it—though now, many other brands have vintage lines.

In three generations, the Weil family has seen the Western business evolve from regional to national then international popularity. Rockmount is proud to be the last of the original Western apparel manufacturers to produce much of its collection in the United States. The Rockmount brand is now sold by 600 retailers worldwide, from saddle shops in Montana to high-fashion boutiques in Los Angeles, London, Paris, and Tokyo, among other fashion capitals.

Rockmount's signature design with "sawtooth" pockets and "diamond" snaps is the longest-running shirt design in America. It was introduced in the late 1940s—originally a slim fit, now relaxed fit—and continues to be made in the USA. It is made in a full range of fabrics, including denim No. 640-DT, shadow plaid No. 693, solid No. 6940, and flannel No. 647.

ROCKMOUNT IN THE MEDIA

While the movies and music influenced Western fashion originally, today Rockmount influences fashion through all types of entertainment worlds, from music to movies and television, and the internet and social media. Rockmount shirts have been worn by Hollywood stars in hundreds of films and shows. We believe our list of musical artists is possibly unequaled. We can even boast a US president, US senators, Colorado governors, and Denver mayors among those who have worn Rockmount. What small business has had this kind of reach and impact on popular culture? We chronicle many visionaries across all aspects of culture in our "Celebrities and Rockmount" chapter (page 45).

Whenever Western apparel makes the news, our brand is often prominently featured. Rockmount has appeared in the *New York Times*, *Wall Street Journal*, *Economist*, *Esquire*, *Vogue*, *GQ*, the *Denver Post*, United Airlines' *Hemispheres*, American Airlines, and American Automobile Association magazines. Many of these articles are syndicated in hundreds of publications.

Three generations represent Rockmount at the Denver Metro Convention & Visitors Bureau Awards in 2007.

Rockmount has been featured in dozens of TV shows, including CNN, *CBS Evening News*, *Jeopardy!*, and *Wheel of Fortune*. Recent shows with Rockmount include *Yellowstone*, *Tulsa King*, *South of the Border*, and *Fresh Off the Boat*.

Rockmount's Denver headquarters is still in the historic landmark building at 1626 Wazee Street in lower downtown (LoDo), where the company has been located since 1946. Rockmount is the last remaining early mercantile business in LoDo's historic district, an area once filled with wholesale businesses. Today, Rockmount's HQ also includes its flagship store and museum, reflecting Americana and Western wear's history and future. The museum has a large collection of vintage Rockmount and Western memorabilia.

We have also received considerable recognition from the City of Denver, including awards for our role in historic preservation and for being a destination site for visitors. Visit Denver, the convention and visitor's bureau, created a national advertising campaign in 2007 featuring Papa Jack on billboards.

Ask For Papa Jack, a billboard featured in Visit Denver's national advertising campaign in 2007.

ROCKMOUNT'S CHALLENGES

As strong as Rockmount's history and brand identity are, the company recognizes the challenges faced by any small business, particularly when the economy is volatile. Typically, starting a business is its greatest challenge. According to the US Bureau of Labor Statistics, 20 percent of startups fail in their first year, and 65 percent within ten years. The Small Business Administration says the succession rate is 30 percent from first- to second-generation businesses, 12 percent to third-generation businesses, and 3 percent to fourth-generation businesses.

However, once a business is established, there are far greater challenges to survival. That said, Rockmount has endured major economic downturns occurring about every decade. At the macroeconomic level, there have been six global recessions since 1970: 1974, 1984, 1990, 1996, 2008, 2018. I credit Papa Jack's conservative financial practices with our resilience during these downturns. His Midwestern sensibilities were shaped by the Great Depression. He avoided debt and retained the company's earnings to power through lean times, a policy we maintain today.

Over the decades, numerous microeconomic factors have shaken the foundations too, and real estate is chief among them. It has not been an easy proposition to remain in our historic building since 1946. Many family businesses get forced out of their locations due to rising real estate values, which can often end a business. My father and I felt our historic building was part of our identity and wanted to do all possible to remain here in LoDo. Although it was counterintuitive, we stayed on Wazee Street when all the other locally owned companies, including several direct competitors, had left. This neighborhood was the birthplace of the city in 1859, when gold was first discovered in the Cherry Creek, which borders our business neighborhood. Later, it became the warehouse district for food, merchandise, and equipment brought by train, starting in the mining days of the late nineteenth century. Denver's downtown has always had a boom-and-bust history, attributed to mining earlier, next oil and gas, then global economic impacts, and most recently the pandemic impact on remote work. Denver's downtown, same as most major markets, has major retail and office vacancies. However, we are very fortunate that Rockmount is a destination that draws retail traffic, exceeding the level before the pandemic. As the city grew eastward in the 1930s, LoDo dissipated and became the city's skid row until the 1990s. It was revitalized in a myriad of ways, including Coors Field being built in 1995 for the Colorado Rockies Major League Baseball team; followed by the construction of nearby Ball Arena for the Colorado Avalanche National Hockey League Team and the Denver Nuggets National Basketball Association team; the Denver Broncos National Football League's stadium being constructed at Empower Field in 2001. Finally, the completed 2014 renovation of Denver Union Station as a regional transit hub tied it all together, including access to Denver International Airport.

Dad and I felt this location was crucial to our future, so we negotiated the purchase of the building with family members not involved in the company. This was an extremely difficult effort, but the opportunity made us reinvent our use of the building, eventually adding a retail store, offices for lease, and a parking garage.

There were other challenges. A major economic crisis happened when I first arrived on the scene; in 1981, the Western fashion industry collapsed when the so-called "Urban Cowboy" fad (1978–81) ended. This was the industry's first boom-and-bust cycle. During the boom, Rockmount had stopped taking orders from new customers to satisfy existing ones. Interest rates were high, and major name brand department stores were slow to pay. Jack A. laid down the law and said no shipments to slow-paying stores, no matter how famous. While Rockmount had been more conservative than other firms in our industry, we had made huge investments in production and were heavily over-inventoried when sales slowed. Other firms had committed to long-term expansion and built new brick-and-mortar factories and retail stores. This kind of overly optimistic thinking, assuming that the spike in business would go on forever, bankrupted hundreds of businesses when the fad ended. While it took years to move Rockmount's excess inventory, the company persevered.

Other macroeconomic trends had massive impacts on domestic manufacturers and retailers. The deluge of cheap Western wear imports has been Rockmount's nemesis and greatest challenge since the 1960s, when US labor rates began to increase significantly in comparison to less-developed countries. However, it was the North American Free Trade Agreement (NAFTA), enacted in 1994, that decimated the US textile and apparel manufacturing industries; less than 5 percent of those factories survived it at the time, fewer today. Yes, the trade-off benefitting consumers with cheaper imported goods meant the loss of the manufacturing sector, which helped create the middle class. The impact of less domestic manufacturing had domino effects, from major job losses in those factory communities to economic losses to their suppliers of all raw materials and losses to government revenue in payroll taxes, property taxes, corporate income taxes, and so on. Rockmount continues to manufacture in the US, but the loss of domestic sources makes operating here more difficult.

Rockmount has always believed that our classic American fashion should be made in America. We fought importing from countries that pay workers per day what is paid per hour in the US, not to mention employee benefits that many US companies provide. Rockmount's distinct identity is strengthened now as the last original domestic manufacturer of Western apparel. Exclusively a domestic manufacturer for sixty years, we simply cannot make everything in the US today due to lower foreign prices, which make US products uncompetitive. Another issue is that the labor force participation rate in the US is about 62 percent, so about 38 percent of able-bodied, working-age people choose not to work. There is a growing labor shortage that makes manufacturing in the US extremely challenging.

After the demise of domestic textile mills, Rockmount began sourcing fabric in India, with its fine textile tradition going back a thousand years. It made sense to also produce our more ornate special treatment shirts there, the ones not feasible to make in the US. So, after fighting the tide of outsourcing abroad, in the 1990s we finally made the difficult decision to begin some foreign manufacturing, not all. This step allowed us to significantly broaden our design range. The rest of the Western industry chose to move all production abroad and simplify designs to reduce prices; other brands abandoned the elaborate shirt designs that originally made the fashion popular from the 1940s to 1960s. However, we maintained our US factories and make all we can here.

Always striving to be distinctive, Rockmount made its name by being countercultural. We continue to produce quality products in the US, but, by establishing artisan production in India, we have revived the golden age special treatments that cannot be made here due to high costs and lost skills. By sticking to our roots and using premium materials and difficult-to-copy special treatments made possible through expert shirtmakers, we continue our tradition of innovation that Papa Jack instilled in Rockmount from day one.

Advertising Easels

I saw one of these in a collection in California and featured it in my *Western Shirts* book. When I saw it, a strange feeling came over me as a distant memory surfaced. It turns out I had seen them as a child puttering around the company. Then, in 2005, during renovation of the Rockmount Building, the architect miscalculated, so we had to remove part of Papa's office for a new stairway. I had a few hours to remove things from his office that had accumulated for decades. Life has a funny way of being serendipitous. I feel like an archaeologist. Hidden in the space between cabinetry and the wall was a stack of four original large cardboard shirt counter cards. We recreated them and now sell them as a series of posters.

Back to the *Western Shirts* book. My grandfather and I did a book talk at a community center in Denver. A lady in the audience had one of these easels in yellow, the fifth version in the series. I asked, "Where did you get that?" She replied, "I was the artist." I about fell over.

Sue Shapiro (1919–2014) was a young artist when Papa hired her, just starting out. She did a lot of graphics for Rockmount in the '40s and '50s but said Papa did not trust her with heads, so she drew everything else.

CHANNELS OF DISTRIBUTION

Back in the 1930s, during the Great Depression, Jack A. started in business by taking out ads in country newspapers, which at the time was a major channels of distribution. The other channel was wholesale. While chain stores emerged in the US in the late nineteenth and early twentieth centuries, Papa disliked their strategy of trading quality for cheap prices. So, he chose a different route. My grandfather instilled in us a commitment to support independent retailers by not discounting to the big discounters, which are considered "category killers" with unfair advantage over small businesses. We extend credit and have a one-price policy, which enables the brand to maintain its integrity and support the US middle class. While we never discount, we sell to major corporations, including many resorts and theme parks such as the Walt Disney Company.

The middle class was built by small business, and today, small business has become an endangered species. Where we once fought big-box discounters, now it's online retailers and Chinese knockoffs—all threats to quality and customer service. We distance ourselves by focusing on quality, unique design, value, and our brand identity.

Today, we've become an unintentional poster child for small business. The fact is, we have survived the massive consolidation of retail that has completely altered the landscape. A fraction of the small, locally owned stores, whether Western or any other category, are still in business. This affects our channel of distribution because we have always supported independent retailers. Also, consolidation has created fewer channels. We once did business with about 2,000 stores in the US and abroad; now, about one third survive. Innovate or stagnate is the choice, and just as we had done in the past, we reinvented—in this case, our channels of distribution.

Counter advertising easels for retailers, 28 inches tall, c. 1940s–50s.

ROCKMOUNT FLAGSHIP STORE

Ironically, we went into retail about the time the sector went on life support. (Remember what I said earlier about us being countercultural?) Thousands of stores were closing throughout every sector of retail, undercut by the advent of discounting retail websites. Where once Walmart had killed locally owned stores where it put stores, Amazon is like a retail pandemic, global. Brick-and-mortar stores in every category from sports to pets to toys to Western wear were gone. So, what did Rockmount do? We established two new channels of distribution: an online presence in 2001 and opened our flagship brick-and-mortar retail store in 2005. This strategy was not price driven but was about fine quality of unique designs. We had never considered selling direct to consumers when there was a thriving retail sector, mainly because we would never compete with our own dealers. But one day, we woke up to a new retail world order that required a change in strategy.

Our first foray into retail was in 2004, when a new shopping mall in the western suburbs of Denver built a store for us. We had also opened a small retail

Rockmount flagship store, Denver.

area in our Wazee Street offices in 2002, but mostly as an afterthought. LoDo was a great location, near the professional sports venues, an entertainment mecca with fine dining, trendy hotels, an exciting nightlife, a strong commercial base, and a growing residential presence. The tiny store was off to the side in what was formerly a small private office, but it did very well. So, in 2005, we decided to grow into real retail and opened our flagship store. We did everything possible to distinguish it from every mall in America. First, it's a 1909 historic building on a prime downtown real estate block. The building is heavily timbered with original hardwood floors; retail fixtures are antiques, wood, leather, and oriental rugs—again, to reflect our sense of history. Above is a beautifully restored fifteen-foot-high pressed tin ceiling. The walls are covered with celebrities photographed in our store or wearing our label. The place feels warm, welcoming, a world apart from generic retail elsewhere. It's been said that good architecture is good for the soul, and we believe that to our core.

Our customers seem to agree; they are intrigued by something they have never seen in a store. Additionally, our direct contact with them gives us a much better pulse on the market, something we did not have in the past. This store is also an incubator and showcase of how we merchandise that we can show our dealers. Our pricing is full retail, and we sell out to the last piece, maintaining the integrity of the brand. Because again, we're not about discounts—we do not compete with our dealers. The store has succeeded, growing every year. And we never know who will walk in the door (see the "Celebrities" chapter, page 45).

ROCKMOUNT ONLINE

We first developed our web presence in 2001 with rockmount.com, mostly for public relations. We launched it as CNN interviewed Papa Jack for his 100th birthday, as the oldest CEO. The website has driven our marketing presence, which is especially important in regions where no Western stores remain. You must change to thrive, or go extinct, as Papa Jack would say. Rockmount.com is a growing channel of distribution worldwide for both wholesale and retail. Given a disrupted retail landscape, we can reach anyone, anywhere from Antarctica to Australia, Paris to Peoria. Our website is filled with our archive of great press coverage and features notable people who wear Rockmount.

Of course, the Web is a two-edged sword. It gets your brand and product out there, but it enables the predatory sites to eat your lunch. We find many Chinese websites that have copied our images and pretend to sell knockoffs at prices below our cost. On the other hand, the Web has, by now, helped level the playing field for small businesses as they struggle against mass marketers. Rockmount reaches the world one person at a time with a click. Papa Jack's lifetime spanned the era from country newspapers to the World Wide Web; his culture of commitment to innovation and change is why Rockmount thrives today.

THE PANDEMIC

Finally, any discussion of existential challenges should include the pandemic. In March 2019, the world as we knew it changed. During the mandatory shutdown, my challenge was to review finances and figure out a financial and operating plan.

One of the things I did from home during the stay-at-home order was to apply for the Paycheck Protection Program (PPP) offered by the federal government to avoid layoffs and help keep employees on the payroll. This was not easy, because our bookkeeper, who was ill with COVID-19, was hospitalized so I couldn't ask for her help. Fortunately, we got the subsidy, the only time in company history that we received funding from the government.

Prior to the launch of PPP, we kept everyone on the payroll for several weeks while they stayed home. We also kept our factories open to the extent allowed by the government. Although sales had dropped to zero, we kept production moving. While I gave this a lot of thought, something my grandfather said in 1975 came back to me. During a serious recession, he'd done a mailing to our retailers and brought up his experience during the Great Depression of 1930s. What he'd learned then were important lessons: don't stop investing in your business; bring in fresh merchandise so customers have a reason to buy; be ready for them when they're ready. So, I did something similar: I committed to keeping our employees both at our headquarters and our factories so we'd be ready when business returned. I'm proud to say that over the decades-long history of Rockmount, our family was never forced to lay off employees. True to Papa Jack's advice and experience, when the pandemic ended, consumer demand exploded. Supporting our people had been the right thing to do. You don't learn this in business school.

In fact, when the pandemic began, we studied the data and came up with and implemented an operating plan to keep staff and customers safe, including biofiltration equipment—constant cleaning. As a result, there were no cases of COVID-19 transmitted in our business.

Although we kept at full production through the pandemic and even now, we have been unable to meet demand as we had done in the past. At this writing, three years after the crisis, our products sell so rapidly, we find it hard to maintain inventory.

When we reopened after the shutdown, a national *NBC News* film crew happened to be filming outside our retail store. They were doing a piece on a retail chain store company that had collapsed during the pandemic. I made it clear that they could not feature our building as a backdrop in that story, to which they agreed. Turns out, their interest in how Rockmount had managed to keep going through the pandemic was piqued, and we landed a profile on how a local business made it through an unparalleled crisis. That media story helped kickstart the business when we reopened.

After COVID-19, another existential challenge hit most every downtown in America: remote work. Rockmount is two blocks from Union Station, a major transit hub. In 2025, city leaders estimate daytime traffic is down 30 to 40 percent. Yet our neighborhood had thrived with little vacancy pre-2019. Today, storefronts and offices are vacant across the country. At Rockmount, we are fortunate; our traffic and sales are up since 2019. As a unique store, we are a destination. Generic homogeneity does not inspire or motivate people. Being countercultural is rooted in the Western lifestyle and ethos. As I often say, who needs another boring shirt?

OPPOSITE: The Rockmount Building, built in 1909.

ABOVE: Jack A, Jack B., and Steve in Rockmount's warehouse, 1995. Courtesy Povy Kendal Atchison.

THE FUTURE

What does the future of Rockmount look like? Who comes after me? Will my son take the Rockmount reins from me? What can we expect over the next few years?

All good questions. We roll with the punches. Innovation is in our DNA. Business remains strong and keeps growing. We have a good relationship with the market. We believe Rockmount can thrive indefinitely if we keep our eye on the ball.

My 27-year-old son, Colter, is deep into his private banking investor career in Los Angeles. Wendy, my wife, had a long career in fashion and works in our store part-time. My goal is to keep doing what I do but balance it with travel, horseback riding, skiing, and other hobbies that inspire me and keep my outlook fresh. My grandfather loved his work and continued doing it until age 107; my father likewise, until 79. Distractions are important because they keep Rockmount fresh and vibrant.

ANATOMY OF A WESTERN SHIRT: DESIGN GENRES & ELEMENTS

For three generations, our family has considered the designing and manufacturing of Rockmount products like an art form. Artisans do our special treatments. Nothing is mass-produced. Humans, not computerized machines, touch everything. While manufacturing techniques have evolved over the years, at root we remain labor-intensive. Much of our collection of silk ties and scarves are collaborations with fine artists, and they are numbered, limited editions. In the shirt arena, we go to great lengths to source and make many of our own fabrics, which helps distinguish our brand. We often innovate with fabrics not generally used in Western shirts or by other brands. We like being edgy, even quirky. We love introducing motifs not generally associated with Western, such as our embroidered rocket ships, stars and planets, and hops designs. Our prints include vintage Western, paniolo Hawaiian, Day of the Dead, and much more. The collaborations with fine artists

Western Wear & Equipment Magazine, 1979, celebrating first issue ad from 1959.

Rockmount catalog, 1963. Jack A's grandsons Greg Romberg (top) in hat and Steve Weil (below) in chaps and vest.

for our silk collection are unique. And our kids' shirt collection has the same expensive special treatments as the adults', which had not been done for youth until we introduced it as a new category.

In the 1940s, when the Western wear industry first emerged, Papa Jack used suiting fabric in the early Western shirts. Back then, there were no suppliers of raw materials for the nascent Western industry. Papa used woolen and rayon gabardines and other premium fabrics in high-quality shirts, which are represented in our archive. Be distinctive was his mantra. In fact, his tag line in the 1940s was "new and different," but it became "distinctive" by the 1950s–1970s.

He took fabrics not in Western use and made them Western, and a defining trademark for Rockmount continues today.

My dad, Jack B., also sourced fabric from mills not generally involved in the Western shirt space. As an artist, Dad knew no boundaries and tried new things every season. After taking over design in the 1950s, he created some wickedly wild designs in every new collection. One of my favorites from the 1960s is the zigzag flame stitch shirt he named "Out of Sight" (see page 43). The notable collection of vintage Rockmount pieces that I started gathering as a teenager now exceeds a thousand pieces. I am highly selective: after all, we can't buy back everything we ever made.

Papa had set an overall design direction from the beginning, emphasizing Rockmount's "distinctive" and "designed in the West by Westerners" taglines. We continue to create design treatments that the other brands never did or ultimately dropped due to rising labor costs. Our shirts to this day have edge stitching, double needling, flap and smile pockets, snaps, longer tails, and sleeve plackets. Indeed, more than forty operations are needed to create one shirt. We love cool singular treatments, such as elaborate contours of yokes, embroidery, and special stitching. Originally, raw materials cost more than the sewing labor; this ratio flipped in the 1960s, and most brands simplified their designs to the point of being generic. Gone were the days of identifying a car by its front grill, and likewise, the same with most shirt brands becoming less distinguishable. Many went to production in developing countries for lower labor costs. Rockmount ignored this trend and stuck to its roots, making it unique.

I based my design direction on the foundation laid by my father and grandfather, and this continuity helps account for our strong following. Our market appreciates authenticity, particularly in a time of generic homogeneity. This is why Rockmount has remained relevant in the fashion world for generations. Three major factors influenced my design direction:

First, my MBA study group influenced me to design for my friends. We met weekly in our showroom to work on school projects. They became an unofficial board of directors and encouraged me to try new fabrics that were not in our collection. We brought back denim, chambray, and Pima cotton solids. (Permanent press blends had dominated shirts since the 1970s.)

Second, and most fundamentally, is my deep appreciation for the design foundation created by my grandfather and father through the 1960s, long since out of production and otherwise lost to posterity. I began reissuing my favorite designs, but with twists that made them appealing to contemporary tastes.

Third, my design skills grew to a new level through collaborations with Japanese trading companies doing business in the best fashion stores in

Rockmount has been making wood signs since the 1940s for stores across the world carrying the brand. The artwork reflects Rockmount's Western ethos and long-term branding. These signs are available for collectors too.

Japan. In the late 1980s, we were approached by various such companies and worked with each on a wide range of designs; these relationships continue today. These partnerships added a creative aesthetic that helped us appreciate our classic roots and also try new things. The important thing here is that Rockmount branched out to a wider fashion audience that appreciates the brand as Americana, adding a new perspective to Western wear. While most brands hit the Japanese market hard for one season and then disappear, we played our cards differently, never saturating the market and carefully selecting distributors with only the top stores, and limiting the number of stores in an area selling our shirts, blankets, and bandanas. Rockmount is the rare brand that has remained popular in Japan for over forty years. The Japanese trading companies appreciate our family business tradition. In fact, our signature bronc T-shirt was a collaboration with one of our distributors, Nobu Hirota from Osaka, who loved the artwork he saw in our 1940s signage on a visit to Rockmount. I had seen it every day, but it was he who encouraged me to translate it into a collection, now in production since the late 1980s. Today, we use the signature bronc design in our vintage embroideries for both adults and kids.

ABOVE: The bronc is an iconic symbol of the American West, and Rockmount has made it a signature design of the brand since the firm was founded. It first appeared in our 1940s signage created for dealers carrying the brand. Today, Rockmount celebrates the West with its ornately embroidered shirts. Fine embroidery, like the craftsmanship in leather tooling on saddles and belts, helped create an identity for the Western way of life. This is central to the popularization of Western fashion.

Shirt Design Genres

In keeping with the art form reference, there have been many genres of design in our shirts since Rockmount began in the 1940s. I consider the 1940s–1960s the Golden Age of Western Wear. We have reintroduced many of these designs from our archives.

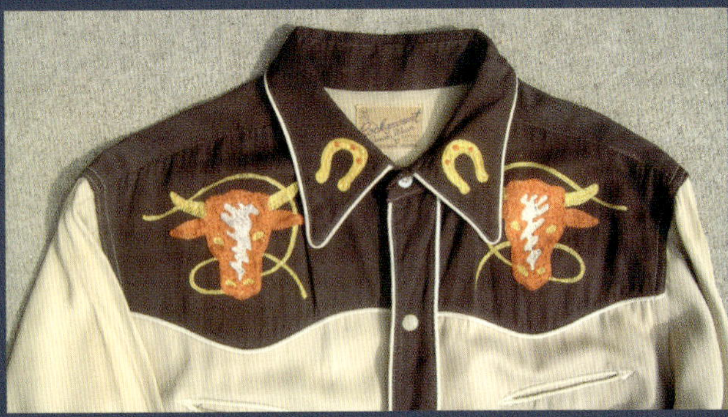

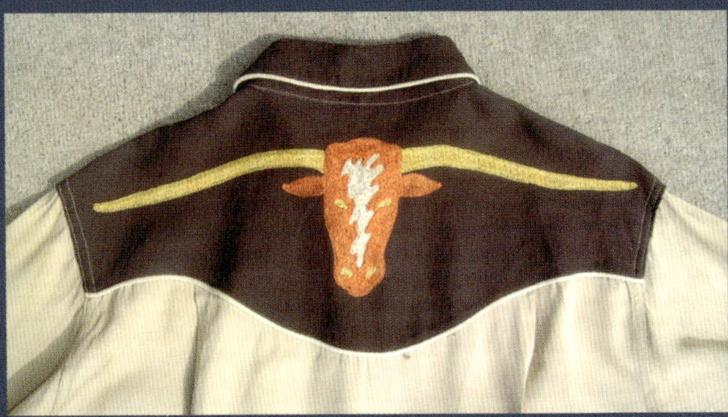

ABOVE: The 1940s classic steer embroidery by Jack A. is back in production for kids today. Note the early enamel style snaps.

RIGHT: This 1950s art deco floral by Jack B. is remade today for men, women, and kids.

The 1950s daily wearable shadow plaids, stripes, denim—timeless and still in production.

The 1960s fashion revolution with "Out of Sight" flame stitch fabric, florals, tie dyes. This look represents a new age in Western design, very much influenced by my father, Jack B.

Contemporary: fleece; Native American-inspired patterns; lifestyle, not costume.

HOLY MACKEREL
89 LB
Ronald Reagan

CELEBRITIES AND ROCKMOUNT

We are their fans, and they are ours!
This is not just name dropping on steroids but stars in our eyes.

Whether they're performing on stage or in film, we love it when creative visionaries wear Rockmount shirts, hats, and accessories; it validates the brand and its design integrity. There is a special beauty when talented artists like what we do, to fit their vibe and enhance stage presence.

My family has always thought of what we do as something more than just business. To us, creative design is an art form, and very much rooted in the integrity of the American West.

Papa Jack, my grandfather, was old school. In addition to the ranchers, farmers, and rodeo markets, he knew there was a demand for a Western identity and romance. He helped create a fashion identity for Westerners. It also appeals to people elsewhere, who identify with the lifestyle. His mission was to bring something new to the landscape.

This never-worn stripe shirt from the 1950s features early rainbow label, one-piece yoke, and pocket flaps, hex snaps; original tags and box.

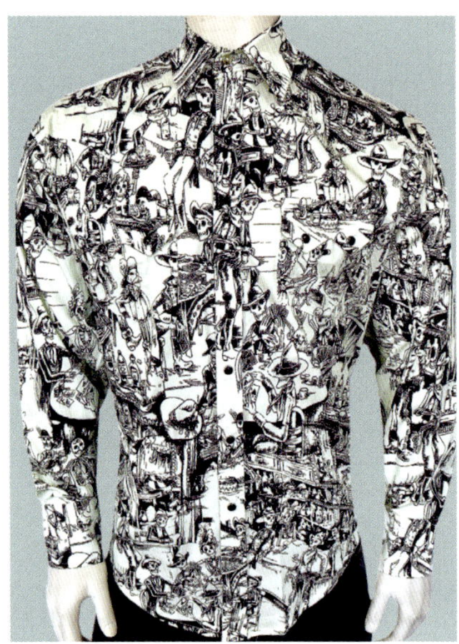

This tradition of innovative design continued with my father, Jack B, who joined his father in 1954. Dad was an artist at heart and was always thinking outside the box to do something different. His designs mirrored the times. His 1950s designs were a total departure from other brands, great embroideries and appliques that were made by artisans.

Somehow, inadvertently, Rockmount developed a following beyond our target market, and it was imperceptible until I joined the company in the 1980s. The three of us—Papa Jack, Jack B, and I—had completely different approaches to our mission, reflecting our different generations. I often told Dad and Papa that if two people in a firm agree on everything, one is not needed.

Still, fundamentally, the three of us shared the DNA of the brand, and its ethos. Where we differed came down to preference, as our roles manifested over time. Papa Jack ran administration and manufacturing, Dad headed design, I did the marketing and advertising. My job was to tell the narrative and build the brand reach and its appeal to my generation. The media has been receptive to our story, which helped greatly in spreading the word and putting it on the public radar. Some of these stories got serious media attention. The Eric Clapton story has had great exposure. It was told in the *Times* of London, the *Denver Post*, and other media. I feel very grateful to have had the opportunity to tell this story. It, and the other stories, help perpetuate the brand and maintain its relevance.

Although the history of Rockmount in film and stage goes back to the 1940s, we only learned it much later. Originally, Rockmount was only sold through stores for over sixty years. We never had direct contact with the retail consumers. The films and musicians bought Rockmount in stores. So, we didn't learn about the celebrity angle until many years later, when we occasionally stumbled across it or were informed by our fans and followers. Later, we began meeting many famous people who wore our brand, an unintended side benefit that began in the

Why do people wear Rockmount? Why is it in the movies and on rock stars? Why does it appear in popular culture?

One word: Americana.

The beauty of Western fashion is that it means different things to different people. It's the Western ethos, it celebrates individuality. It's also timeless. Grandfathers and granddaughters wear Rockmount Ranch Wear, as do Republicans and Democrats. From cowboys to cowgirls, lawyers to coders, doctors to truck drivers, Rockmount was born All American but has also gone international. Few genres in fashion have this diverse following; even fewer, its longevity. How we maintain that following long term is an existential challenge. It's in the DNA.

1980s, when the power of pop culture was exploding. Many of the people we met shared a private side of their personality and were gracious and kind.

The following chapter includes famous people we met—and some we did not—who wear Rockmount. We began meeting most of them after two important developments:

First, when rockmount.com was created in 2001, we began hearing from the most interesting people. My goal was to have the website up in time for my grandfather's 100th birthday and an upcoming CNN interview of a 100-year-old businessman.

The second important development was opening our flagship Denver store in 2005. Many people think the Rockmount store has been here forever, but we were wholesale only until 2001. So, until then, the movies bought Rockmount at stores carrying our line, often in the Los Angeles area. Musicians bought it from stores across the country and abroad. We were unaware of our prevalence in films and music until later years, when we and others began to see it worn by celebrities. Also, being online made it much easier for wardrobe people and artists to contact us to buy Rockmount. We are also most appreciative of our fans, who found it easier to let us know online and by email when they saw Rockmount in stage performances, films, and TV. When they sent photos, we accumulated a massive collection, many of which are included in our archive at rockmount.com. Later, we began meeting the celebrities online and

OPPOSITE:

LEFT: Jack A.'s 1940s solid satin shirt with smile pockets, Bakelite shank buttons (predating snaps), piping.

CENTER: Jack B.'s 1950s pink floral men's shirt with slash pockets, red saddle stitching, black diamond snaps.

RIGHT: Steve's contemporary cowboy pirate print with sawtooth pockets, black snaps.

ELVIS

In August 1977 I was driving from Denver to Tulane University in New Orleans to start my sophomore year and stopped by our factory in Fort Smith, Arkansas. From there I drove through Memphis, when the traffic on the highway came to a halt. Elvis had died. It was eerie, one of those strange moments in life that never leaves you. I had no idea that it would later have a pivotal impact on both me and our company.

Many years later, while on business in Dallas, I watched a 25th anniversary retrospective of Elvis's career and legacy. So, there I was, when I saw clips of Elvis in the movie *Love Me Tender* (1956). He wore a Western shirt, and it caught my attention. It was a burgundy windowpane check with sawtooth pockets. In the 1950s, Rockmount was only sold through our retail dealer network; there were no direct sales. I realized that the shirt was probably bought at a Rockmount dealer.

As the self-appointed explorer of family history, I used to go through the considerable pile of trunks in our warehouse that held family memorabilia dating from my great-grandparents to my dad's US Army trunk, left there in 1954 when he returned to Denver to join his father's firm. The trunk had a 1950s Rockmount burgundy check shirt that was identical to the one Elvis wore!

OPPOSITE: Several years ago while at MAGIC, the largest men's apparel trade show, we met the family who runs Lansky's store in Memphis. Like us, they are a three-generation firm, and they supplied Elvis with his wardrobe. Together, we collaborated to remake our shirt No. 67-ELV, worn by "The King of Rock 'n' Roll" in the 1957 film *Loving You;* he sings "Let Me Be Your Teddy Bear," while wearing the red and white two-tone with floral embroidery, continuing in production now.

ABOVE: Elvis in *Loving You.* Courtesy Elvis Presley Enterprises & Graceland.

Upon returning home from the Dallas trip, I headed to the warehouse and found the shirt. It had a special Rockmount label co-branded with Dan River Fabric. Dan River was a major textile firm supplying much of our fabric from the 1940s until 1992, when NAFTA (the North American Free Trade Agreement) would kill the US domestic textile industry. Papa had started the relationship with Dan River, and Dad built it up with regular visits to the company's New York City offices. I joined him as we sourced fabrics for each year's collection. During one particular visit there, I asked them to recreate the burgundy fabric so we could remake the Elvis shirt. They agreed, surprising the young kid.

I took the remake to MAGIC in Las Vegas, the largest men's fashion trade show in the world. Papa was skeptical that the high cost of exhibiting would be worth it, because Rockmount is in the Western market niche and would be swallowed up by the overall fashion trade show world. However, we had steadily developed our Japanese, European, and Australian business, and many of those customers would see us there along with new stores from outside our world. (This trade show helped grow our business over the years we attended, from 1988 until the pandemic hit in 2019.)

Wouldn't you know, our remake of Elvis's burgundy check shirt sold out before the production was finished! It was my first home run, and Graceland agreed to let us use the photo in my first book.

It was one of those "aha" moments: if Elvis wore Rockmount, other famous people in film and stage might have, too. This prompted me to start an archive by collecting photos of Rockmount in the movies. Among the first we discovered were early movies such as *The Misfits*, the 1961 film with Cary Grant and Marilyn Monroe. The archive now goes all the way through hundreds of films up to the present day. The archival photos of stage and screen are on display at Rockmount, covering much of the wall space.

This 1950s shirt matches the one worn by Elvis in *Love Me Tender*. Jack B had left it in his US Army foot locker when he started at Rockmount in 1954.

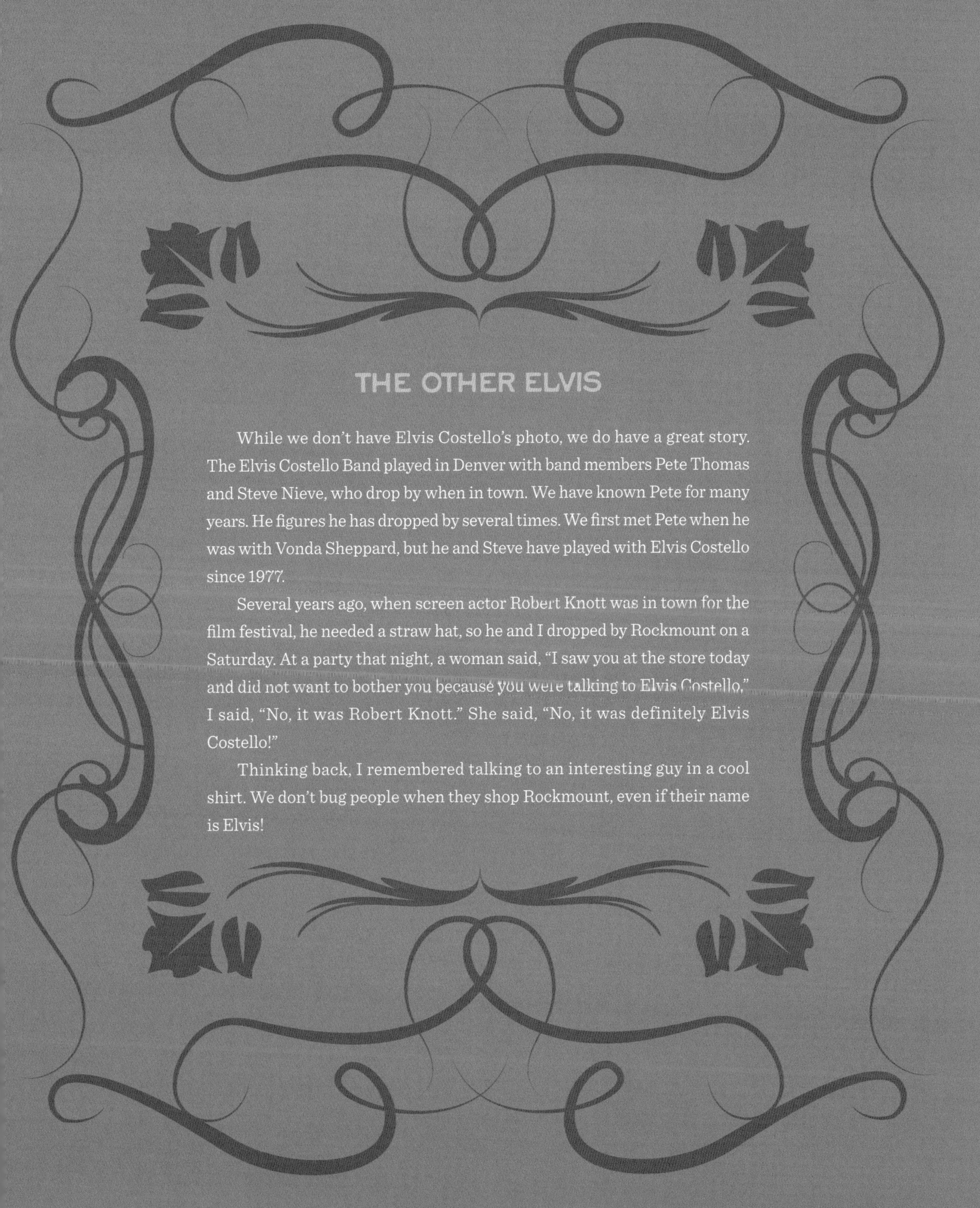

THE OTHER ELVIS

While we don't have Elvis Costello's photo, we do have a great story. The Elvis Costello Band played in Denver with band members Pete Thomas and Steve Nieve, who drop by when in town. We have known Pete for many years. He figures he has dropped by several times. We first met Pete when he was with Vonda Sheppard, but he and Steve have played with Elvis Costello since 1977.

Several years ago, when screen actor Robert Knott was in town for the film festival, he needed a straw hat, so he and I dropped by Rockmount on a Saturday. At a party that night, a woman said, "I saw you at the store today and did not want to bother you because you were talking to Elvis Costello." I said, "No, it was Robert Knott." She said, "No, it was definitely Elvis Costello!"

Thinking back, I remembered talking to an interesting guy in a cool shirt. We don't bug people when they shop Rockmount, even if their name is Elvis!

ERIC CLAPTON

Our first personal movie connection came about with the 1993 modern Western, neo-noir thriller film *Red Rock West*, while our first rock star connection was with Eric Clapton. I had no idea how this kind of "brush with greatness" would accelerate our fame and become a part of regular life at Rockmount. There is something special about going to work in the morning with no idea how the day will transpire.

People ask me all the time why rock stars have a propensity for Rockmount. It's kind of hard to say what motivates people—especially visionaries—but this passage from Clapton on Americana in the June 2, 2016, edition of *Rolling Stone* magazine sums it up nicely.

My point of reference was zero. I grew up in an English village where we didn't even have a train station. Then I came to New York with Cream to play the Murray the K show, and I saw first-hand all this stuff I was hearing about all my life. To walk around Manhattan as a 20-year-old—it was magical. You would see someone with a biker jacket or cowboy boots; I was in heaven.

Everywhere we went was different. The more I would come back, everywhere started to look the same—the fast-food places, the franchising. Everything got blanded out. It's all gone—to where, I don't know.

Eric Clapton sent me the photo on the left in 2005 (taken by his wife) to show me the shirt he wanted in additional colors. This led to our collaborating on the shirt above.

A TRUE STORY

One evening, April 29, 2005, as I was getting ready to go home for the weekend, I received an email that at first glance seemed risky, but I clicked anyway.

It came from Lord something or other and said:

hi.....

i recently bought some of your shirts from a friend of mine who owns a store called "american classics" on kings road, in chelsea, england and was knocked out....i have always loved real western clothes, and have found [it] increasingly harder to find them even though i have toured extensively across the states for the last forty years ....

would it be possible to order some things from your website, and then have them shipped here to the u.k.? ....i would be so grateful, and obviously i would cover all the costs......please let me know what you think......

all the best, eric clapton

p.s. i realize that you probably would assume that this was a bogus email, and in that eventuality, i am including my office phone number in the u.k. . . . it would be answered by either vivien or cecil, my assistants, who will endeavour to prove to you, that i am who i say i am....the number is; +44 xxxxxxxxx

i realize that this could be a longshot, but you would make an old english rocker very happy..........

– e.c.

I was stunned but knew immediately it was the real deal, and I called my wife Wendy to tell her I would be late for dinner because I needed to reply to ERIC CLAPTON! Wendy's sage advice: "Don't be wordy."

I reduced my reply to a single page and emailed back to say how nice it was to hear from him and that when I was in high school I had heard him play at the historic Oxford Hotel, a cool old place, now restored in Denver's Union Station district across the street from Rockmount.

I went home and asked Wendy if she wanted to see his email. By the time I got home, Eric Clapton had already replied, 2 a.m. London time. Thus began a series of forty or more emails about Rockmount shirts. I bet the printed emails could be a book over an inch thick.

"Slow hand," the rock star icon asked all kinds of questions about the shirts, colors, fit, and design details. He even sent a photo taken by his wife to show off his new black Rockmount shirt No. 640.

So, he ordered sixteen shirts Monday, which we shipped that day.

On Tuesday he ordered more shirts and said, "I want to wear these at the Cream Reunion Concert at the Royal Albert Hall in London on Friday."

I replied, "UPS delivery from the US to UK takes 5 to 7 days. The only way the shirts will arrive in time is if I hand-deliver them myself."

Clapton replied,

> *my kinda guy !.........anyhow, yes, i can get tickets, and if not, i'll smuggle you in the boot of my car !...either way i'll get you in....i was actually hoping that the consignment you sent on Monday might arrive by the last show...but hand delivery sounds even better...*
>
> *it would be good, and probably very helpful for you to get in touch with one or both of my assistants about this...their info...vivien xxxxx + 44 xxxxxxxx and cecil xxxxx + 44 xxxxx...and i have forwarded your last email to both of them....*
>
> *see you Friday? eric c.*

So, I called Gerry Engle, a buddy of mine from business school, a drummer and the only guy I know who would drop everything and fly to London. We made arrangements to leave on the evening flight the next day. Wendy was on a trip and couldn't go with us.

We arrived in London Friday morning, jet lagged and worried: I sobered up enough to realize we had never actually spoken to anyone about the order or the concert. Could it be bogus? This was a time when cell phone roaming charges were astronomical, so exiting the Kensington tube station from Heathrow, I went directly to a bank of pay phones to call. (I had to try several before finding one that worked.) Several tries later, the call went through, and to my great relief someone answered and said, "Good, we are expecting you. Meet us at Royal Albert Hall at 6 p.m. Use the talent's side door."

We arrived early that evening and were ushered backstage to the greenroom to meet Clapton and his family. We talked, had a meal, and I gave him some shirts and my book, *Western Shirts: A Classic American Fashion*. He signed my shirt and we took photos.

We attended the concert and were seated in the front.

Afterwards, we went back to the greenroom and stopped in our tracks in the doorway. There were only a few people there: Paul McCartney, Ringo, Bill Wyman, Tom Hanks. Stunned. Tom Hanks walks over and introduces himself. "Hi, I'm Tom." We introduced ourselves and talked with Tom for half an hour. He was there working on *The Da Vinci Code*. I later asked if I could take a photo, to which Tom said fine. I tapped the closest person on the shoulder to see if he would take the photo. He turned, it was Ringo. Everyone laughed as Ringo shot the photo.

ABOVE: Cream Reunion Concert, Royal Albert Hall, London, with Ginger Baker, Jack Bruce, and Eric Clapton in Rockmount 640 solid shirt, 2005.

RIGHT: Steve Weil, Eric Clapton, and Gerry Engle before the concert.

OPPOSITE: Cream Concert program, tickets, and Rockmount No. 6940, like the one he wore, signed by Eric Clapton.

Scene
The Denver Post
2F The Denver Post ★
BILL HUSTED
Denver Post Staff Columnist
Western shirt just the ticket for Clapton
Rockmount Ranch Wear's Steve Weil is just back from London and Friday night's closing Cream concert at Royal Albert Hall. He flew over on a moment's notice to bring some of his famous Western shirts to Eric Clapton, who had requested them via e-mail. Weil wrote back that he could hand-deliver them, but how 'bout two tix to the concert? Done deal.
"It was incredible," said Weil, still jet lagged and loopy Wednesday morning.
were in row seven, the band was flawless.
And Eric (Clapton) is living art."
Clapton met Weil before the concert to
the shirt and thank him for the extra effort.
After the concert, Weil returned to the
room, where he walked in with Ringo Starr,
Paul McCartney and Bill Wyman.
TRU-WEST
2005
CREAM
FRIDAY
VIP
CREAM
ROYAL ALBERT HALL
Fri, 06 May 2005
At 8:00 PM
Doors open at 7:00 PM
HALL

To Jack Weil
With best wishes, Ronald Reagan

RONALD REAGAN

Papa Jack was friends with the late Malcolm Baldridge Jr., US Secretary of Commerce in the Reagan administration. However, Papa had strongly objected to President Reagan's comments that the service economy had replaced manufacturing in the US, because Papa believed that manufacturing built this country and that this fundamental economic driver was being exported due to bad political policy. Papa wrote that in a letter to Reagan. Baldridge delivered the letter to the president, who responded.

In 1986, Papa said, "When Reagan was elected, he started talking about a 'service economy.' I wrote him that when I was growing up in Evansville, Indiana, only 100 miles from where he [Reagan] grew up in Dixon, Illinois, 'servicing' was what happened when we took the mare to stud."

Reagan replied to Papa in a letter: "Dixon, IL is a long way from Washington, DC."

Still, after Papa received the Western Apparel Industry's Pioneer Award in 1986, President Reagan congratulated him and sent this photo, which is in our archive.

OPPOSITE: Papa carrying the photo that President Reagen sent him.

ABOVE: President Reagan wearing Rockmount at his ranch. Photo courtesy of the Ronald Reagan Presidential Library.

ABOVE: President Reagan with US Navy Seabees, 1981. Photo courtesy of the Ronald Reagan Presidential Library.

OPPOSITE: President Reagan riding at his ranch. Photo courtesy of the Ronald Reagan Presidential Library.

AIDAN QUINN

In the film *Practical Magic*, with Sandra Bullock, Nicole Kidman, Dianne Wiest, and Stockard Channing, star Aidan Quinn wore an iconic Rockmount denim shirt No. 640-DS in the film where he plays a Western lawman who stumbles into friendly witch country in the Northeast. The shirt is the longest production shirt in America and is as closely tied to Rockmount as the model 501 jeans are to that other company. Apparently, Quinn liked the shirt enough to keep it and wear in public over the years, including while visiting Denver with his late brother Paul. We also have seen other images of him wearing Rockmount plaids.

Movie photos courtesy Warner Bros.

NICHOLAS CAGE & DENNIS HOPPER IN *RED ROCK WEST*

In 1993, the costume designer for the movie *Red Rock West* called us to say she was in town to pick up Western wear from other brands, including two brands—which will remain nameless—that had given her a car trunk full of shirts. She said she was staying downtown at the Oxford Hotel, across the street from Rockmount, and asked if we would also like to give her free wardrobe.

I suggested that she stop by and said, "Why don't you come over and see why you will want to actually pay for Rockmount shirts and not use any of the free merchandise from the other companies." It didn't take long for her to come to the same conclusion, and she ended up giving the free shirts to a homeless shelter. This was the first time we had worked with a movie production directly for wardrobe purposes.

In *Red Rock West*, both Nicholas Cage and Dennis Hopper wore Rockmount. My favorite scene is when Nicholas Cage drives around Wyoming in a massive old Cadillac for a job interview. He pulls over to the roadside and opens the Caddy's trunk to put on his nice shirt. The entire screen fills with the Rockmount label!

Thus began our work with hundreds of movies and TV shows, from *Brokeback Mountain* to *Yellowstone*. None of these were pay-to-play by Rockmount. Being chosen by the studio is so much more meaningful to the brand than paid product placement.

Movie photo of Nicholas Cage in *Red Rock West*. Courtesy of Propaganda Films & Polygram Film Entertainment.

ROBERT PLANT

One day in October 2010, near store closing time, I was driving home when my phone rang. Heidi Alfonso from our store asked me, "Can you come back to Rockmount? ROBERT PLANT IS IN THE STORE!"

I screeched on the car brakes and spun around, heading straight back. After all, it's not every day that LED ZEPPELIN is in the building!

And there was no mistaking the smiling man with the lion's mane. As I entered the front door he bellowed: "I am so excited in here!"

That welcoming comment made it easy for a mere mortal to walk over and introduce myself.

I'm not joking when I say the man was beaming like a kid in a candy store. He tried on several shirts and a leather jacket, then took each one to the counter. After waiting what seemed an eternity, I asked if he'd allow us to take photos. He graciously agreed.

Meantime, we talked about history and literature. He mentioned how he loved Texas history and had lived in Austin for a time. His prose and manner were amusing and refreshing; there was no pretense. Plant said he had been coming to Denver for over forty years, noting how much it had changed. Then, as if yesterday, he said he played here on December 26, 1968. Surprised by his recall, I asked him, "How can you remember the exact date?" He answered, "Because it was the opening concert on my first USA tour." Heidi, from our team, mentioned she was thirteen years old when she went to that concert. The band was then the New Yardbirds; they changed their name later to Led Zeppelin. They had started the tour as opening act for Vanilla Fudge and Iron Butterfly, but, according to Jimmy Page, by the time they reached San Francisco, they had eclipsed both of the headline acts.

Plant kindly invited us to the concert the next day at Denver's Fillmore Auditorium, and it was mind-blowing. When we met again the day following, he mentioned he had studied to become a chartered accountant. He invited us again to the concert for the second night. At the concert he said to the audience that he had figured out that it had been "16,718 days since the first time he played Denver." It occurred to me he's not just a rock star but a numbers man.

On the second visit Plant brought the band with him back to Rockmount and was like the friend you take shopping to give you advice. He helped pick a hat No. 1842 for Juldeh Camara (plays a West African lute, the kologo), and a charcoal wool flannel shirt for Justin Adams (on guitar), among others.

Plant paid close attention to all the details and enjoyed some banter.

At the concert after-party, I talked to two band members who lived in Bristol, England, where I had studied law. Keyboard player John Baggot, from Bristol, wore a vintage Rockmount black shirt No. 640 onstage. He also picked up a black leather shirt No. 6666. During the party, Plant asked me what time we open Sundays. I replied, "What time do you need us to open?" All said, he visited three times over three days.

We even got a chance to go out for breakfast. It's a rare moment to meet someone famous and successful, particularly a rock star, who remains friendly, gracious, and grounded.

Interestingly, Plant had bought Rockmount shirts earlier, in Chicago at Alcala's Western Wear on Chicago Avenue. They have carried Rockmount since the 1980s. Rockmount is built on good relationships with our retailers, and we work hard to support them. Our friend Richard Alcala, head of the store, told me that in 2001 Plant had bought one of our early vintage remakes, a two-tone in brown/gold with "smile" pockets and signature "diamond" snaps, like the one at right.

OPPOSITE LEFT: Robert Plant band members Juldeh Camara (ritti and kologo) and John Baggot (keyboards).

OPPOSITE RIGHT: Robert Plant trying on a suede leather jacket.

BORN TO RUN BOSS WALK-IN

Happily, we can share more rock star stories with an Alcala's connection. The number one Western store in the Midwest attracts many of the world's boldest names. In December 1988, while on a flight somewhere, reading *Esquire* magazine, I noticed on the cover was Bruce Springsteen wearing a Western shirt and bolo tie. Looking closely, I recognized Rockmount's concho bolo tie. I followed up with the magazine and they told me it was purchased at Alcala's—small world. They sent me a box of the issue, and we made a collage, which is displayed at Rockmount.

Our Bruce Springsteen connection spans his entire career. We have photos of him wearing Rockmount every decade beginning with his debut album cover *Greetings From Asbury Park, NJ* in 1973.

Springsteen visited Rockmount on March 1, 2023, while on tour. A few years earlier, Springsteen had walked in the Rockmount door, but an overzealous fan had chased him off. During the later visit, though, he was not bothered by anyone and spent a leisurely time with us.

Our team spent about two hours with him shopping and he could not have been nicer. He picked two shirts: No. 621 vintage shadow plaid from our 1950s archive and a Native American pattern fleece shirt No. 6100-RB. His baby granddaughter got a signature bronc onesie. He also selected a horsehair bracelet. We gave him a 75th Anniversary Rockmount medallion, and he invited all of us to the concert—front stage!

The afterglow of meeting Bruce Springsteen and attending his concert ran hot. The concert was among my top two ever. The other was Cream Reunion.

We have seen Springsteen in Rockmount over the years, same for band member Steven Van Zandt. When organizing the photos from his visit and concert, I reviewed our archive and then realized that Springsteen has worn Rockmount his whole career.

Coincidentally, he wears our signature denim with sawtooth pockets and diamond snaps, which is the longest production shirt in the USA. On the 1984 album cover of *Born in the U.S.A.*, Springsteen wears a very cool vintage studded and tooled Rockmount belt. He also wore Rockmount on the album with John Fogerty when he released *Magic* in 2007.

In a *60 Minutes* interview on Oct. 7, 2007, CBS correspondent and anchor Scott Pelley interviewed Bruce Springsteen. Pelley wore a Rockmount denim in the interview. We corresponded later, he told me he has many Rockmount shirts and is a big fan.

CBS correspondent Steve Hartman interviewed Papa Jack, so I wrote him. Here is the correspondence:

> *From: Hartman, Steve*
> *To: Pelley, Scott*
> *Sent: Mon Oct 08 17:14:58 2007*
> *Subject: Shirt*
>
> *Not long ago I did a story about the country's oldest working CEO—103-yrs! He started a company called Rockmount and basically invented the western shirt as we know it. Last night with Bruce (great story by the way) you were wearing one of his designs. His grandson called with 2 requests: 1) Where did you get it? 2) Can they get a digital screen grab for their website. He tells me you'd be pictured with the likes of Clapton and Elvis.*
>
> *Steve Hartman*

> *From: Pelley, Scott*
> *To: Hartman, Steve*
> *Sent: Mon Oct 08 17:25:56 2007*
> *Subject: Re: Shirt*
>
> *Steve I'd be delighted. I've been buying Rockmount shirts from the Denver store for many years. I have a wardrobe of them. Jane wants me to throw out the ones with holes in them but I refuse. . . .*
>
> *I often give Rockmount Ranch Wear as gifts. Send me the e-mail address and I'll send the grab.*
>
> *All best, Scott*

> *From: Pelley, Scott*
> *Sent: Monday, October 08, 2007 7:35 PM*
> *To: Mann, Jan T.*
> *Subject: Fw: Shirt*
>
> *Here is the photo you requested. Hope you enjoy it as much as Scott enjoys your shirts.*
>
> *Jan*
>
> *CBS News*

Photo courtesy Scott Pelley and CBS *60 Minutes*.

Springsteen is not only well spoken but thoughtful about his life and times. Consider this from the *60 Minutes* interview reflecting the responsibility that comes from success:

> *... I'm interested in what it means to live in America. I'm interested in the kind of country that we live in and leave our kids. I'm interested in trying to define what that country is. I got the chutzpah or whatever you want to say to believe that if I write really good about it, it's going to make a difference.*

Bruce said at Superbowl 2021: "We need to find our way back to the middle and reunite."

Another Springsteen comment from a McKinsey & Company article in 2014 especially resonates with me:

> *Getting an audience is hard. Sustaining an audience is hard. It demands a consistency of thought, of purpose, and of action over a long period of time....*
>
> *Things that are bigger than us, connect us. This applies to what we listen to and even wear.*

It took Rockmount decades of creative designs, hard work, and consistent messaging to reach the market we have today.

We also enjoy hearing from fans when they see Rockmount on stage and screen. Sometimes they even make it happen, as when Dan and Michelle Sawyer of Denver went to New York to see "Bruce Springsteen on Broadway" in March 2018. The couple wrote us that they visited Rockmount to get a new shirt for the trip and decided to "get a shirt for Bruce as well."

They said, "At the end of the show Bruce stood and thanked the audience for a few minutes. Michelle went up to the stage and handed him the gift. She said to him, "It's a Rockmount," and Bruce got a big grin. Then he held it up to show the entire crowd.

Dan added, "I've loved wearing your shirts for years. I always look cool and get many compliments. I remember back in the day talking to your grandfather and Sammy from Miami for an hour or so. (Sam Kornblatt worked with Papa from the 1930s and later at Rockmount until he retired at age ninety-three.)

I could not be prouder that people like what we do. And it doesn't hurt that The Boss has worn Rockmount for more than fifty years.

BROKEBACK MOUNTAIN

Brokeback Mountain (2005) was pivotal in the American Western film ethos. The screenplay was by Larry McMurtry based on a short story by a Pulitzer Prize–winning novelist Annie Proulx, directed and acted by A-listers. The controversial film forged a new path in the Western genre, and we played a role outfitting the main characters.

It started when a costume designer called and said that director Ang Lee wanted Rockmount shirts, hats, and accessories for the cast in a movie starring Heath Ledger and Jake Gyllenhaal in the lead roles. Anne Hathaway and Maggie Gyllenhaal are also in the movie. (As a lifelong McMurtry fan, I was all in.)

I said, "Sure."

She said, "But there is something you need to know about the movie. . . ."

I said, "Let me get this straight: Ang Lee wants Rockmount shirts for his next movie?"

She said, "Yes."

I said, "That's good enough for me."

They bought dozens of shirts, hats, and accessories for many of the actors. We were proud to be part of it.

They invited my wife, Wendy, and me to a premier, where we met screenwriters McMurtry and Diana Ossana; the book's author, Annie Proulx; and the cast. After the movie we were invited to a private dinner.

Later, the *Wall Street Journal* interviewed me, asking, "How bad is this movie for business and the Rockmount brand?"

I replied, "Are you kidding? Rockmount has been in hundreds of movies and this is the latest. It is a work of art by Annie Proulx, Larry McMurtry, Ang Lee, with Heath Ledger, Jake Gyllenhaal, Anne Hathaway, and Maggie Gyllenhaal." Why would that be bad for business?

Still, because it involved the portrayal of a gay relationship, we had no idea what the outcome would be. I discussed it with my MBA study group—my unofficial board of directors going back to the 1980s and a good sounding board. The view was to wait to publicize our role. Of course, we had no idea this film would catch fire.

So, after the eighth Academy Award nomination—the movie would win Oscars for Best Director (Ang Lee), Best Original Screenplay (Larry McMurtry and Diana Ossana), and Best Original Score (Gustavo Santaolalla)—we publicized our role in the film and came out of the closet!

Interestingly, we got one piece of hate mail. But overwhelmingly, the public supported our role. Older friends from a historians group I have belonged to for many years had not yet seen the movie but told me they were happy that we played a part in the production. Who knew the movie would help pave the way for more mainstream LGBTQ representation, and perhaps a major shift in public acceptance?

OPPOSITE: Jake Gyllenhaal and Heath Ledger wear Rockmount shirts that were central to the plot—denim No. 0369 and a plaid. (Why is there no Oscar for Best Supporting Shirts?) In fact, those two shirts were later sold at a charity auction for $101,000. This was good value appreciation, considering the studio paid $40 each wholesale.

TOP: Anne Hathaway in *a studio shot.*

BELOW, LEFT TO RIGHT: Actors Doug Sadler and Robert Knott, writer Annie Proulx, and Steve Weil at a cocktail party before the movie premier.

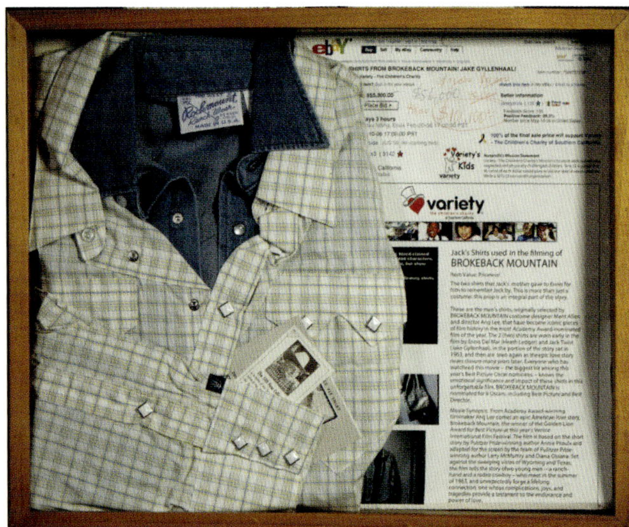

The two shirts have been on long-term exhibit at the Autry Museum of the American West, in Los Angeles. We have this replica of the important door scene at the end of the movie on permanent display in Rockmount's Museum at our flagship store.

Good stories have sequels. I am an avid Larry McMurtry fan. His 1982 book *Cadillac Jack* inspired me to begin a museum collection of our historical designs, memorabilia, and advertising. (Reading McMurtry was one of the best one-sided personal relationships I have ever had.)

Collecting old Western wear was a bizarre idea as recently as the 1980s when McMurtry wrote *Cadillac Jack*—about an itinerant rare antiquities dealer with a penchant for old cowboy boots—I had never heard of anyone else collecting early Western wear until then. The protagonist, somewhat biographical, raised the boots to an art form when taking them to Washington, DC, for a gallery exhibit.

I had begun collecting early Rockmount shirts while in high school in the 1970s because I thought they had historical merit, even though it was not a genre yet. *Cadillac Jack* helped me name my collection of early Rockmount shirts and memorabilia "vintage," eventually leading to my first book, *Western Shirts*, which led to this one. Yet its impact was greater: my admiration of my grandfather's and father's early, groundbreaking designs inspired my design direction and remains rooted all these years later.

We rarely meet our heroes, but this happened at the *Brokeback Mountain* premier. When Larry McMurtry died in 2021, I wrote an essay for our blog:

It's both rare and special to meet one's heroes. We first met (if reading is meeting) through his litany of my favorite books and movies. Our one-way friendship began in 1971 as a teenager seeing the movie The Last Picture Show. . . . *Later there was* Terms of Endearment.

*Jeff Bridges starred in two films based on McMurtry novels—*The Last Picture Show *and* Texasville. *He, his father, Lloyd Bridges, and brother, Beau Bridges, all wore Rockmount denim shirts in an* Esquire *feature.*

Lonesome Dove, *which won McMurtry a Pulitzer Prize in 1986, may be the best Western ever written and filmed. It is considered to be the most popular Western ever made.*

Over the years, I've read everything I could find by McMurtry.

Many of his stories are contemporary Westerns, including The Last Picture Show, *later adapted for the 1971 movie directed by Peter Bogdanovich and starring Jeff Bridges, Cybill Shepherd, Timothy Bottoms, and Cloris Leachman.*

My essay on the Rockmount blog drew one piece of hate mail written by someone who mistakenly called him a cinematographer, but I replied anyway because my tribute had drawn a response from Larry's writing partner, Diana Ossana. We later spoke and she gave us permission to share it.

Diana Ossana wrote:

Hello ~ thank you for your lovely tribute to Larry McMurtry. We were best friends for 36 years and writing partners for 28 years. We co-wrote two novels and 40 screenplays. We co-wrote the screenplay for Brokeback Mountain *after I convinced Larry to read the short story—he didn't read short fiction because he said he couldn't write short fiction, but nonetheless he read it and agreed to write it with me when I asked him. I was on set as the film's producer for the entire production and had urged our production designer to contact Rockmount for wardrobe. The clothing became iconic after the film entered international culture as a touchstone.*

Again, thank you for your tribute. There is no one like Larry. There will never be anyone like Larry. I will miss him forever.

All good things,

Diana Ossana

Photo courtesy *Esquire*.

THIS PAGE: Three photos of Robert Knott wearing Rockmount, at Rockmount. Top, he is with Papa Jack.

OPPOSITE: Papa Jack, Xander Berkeley (in Rockmount), and me at Rockmount.

XANDER BERKELEY AND ROBERT KNOTT

Back in the dark ages (2002), before we did retail, a movie was being shot in Denver, and the leading actors stayed across the street at the Oxford Hotel. Both had played cowboys in various movies and somehow stumbled into Rockmount.

We met daily for morning coffee for a couple of weeks. Xander actually helped me decorate the storefront windows. Back then, the old neighborhood was down and out from years of neglect, but it was beginning to come alive. Help like that doesn't come easily. I must add that I can't shake his performance in the movie *Air Force 1* with Harrison Ford when he played a rogue Secret Service agent.

Robert Knott has stayed in touch over the years. He works with actor, writer, director, and producer Ed Harris and appears in many Westerns, including *Appaloosa*, which resonates with me for more reasons than that my horse growing up was the smartest horse I ever knew and also an amazing Appy! Knott and I reconnected at the premier of *Brokeback Mountain* and later at the Denver Film Festival (both stories told in this chapter).

GRATEFUL DEAD

We have some stories to share about the Dead, although they say if you can remember the 1960s, you weren't there. The band, in 2013, collaborated with us on a series of shirts with their iconography, and the shirts sold out quickly. We have also seen early photos of Jerry Garcia wearing Rockmount denim shirts.

When people hear about our connection to the band, many have their own Dead stories. Some members of our Rockmount team, now retired, at one time toured with the band, and did babysitting and other work for them. It's hard to find anyone who never heard them in concert. Our relationship continued over many years when Phil Lesh visited us.

THE OFFICIAL GRATEFUL DEAD SHIRT
Limited Edition No 40
TM & © 2013 GDP
Rockmount Ranch Wear

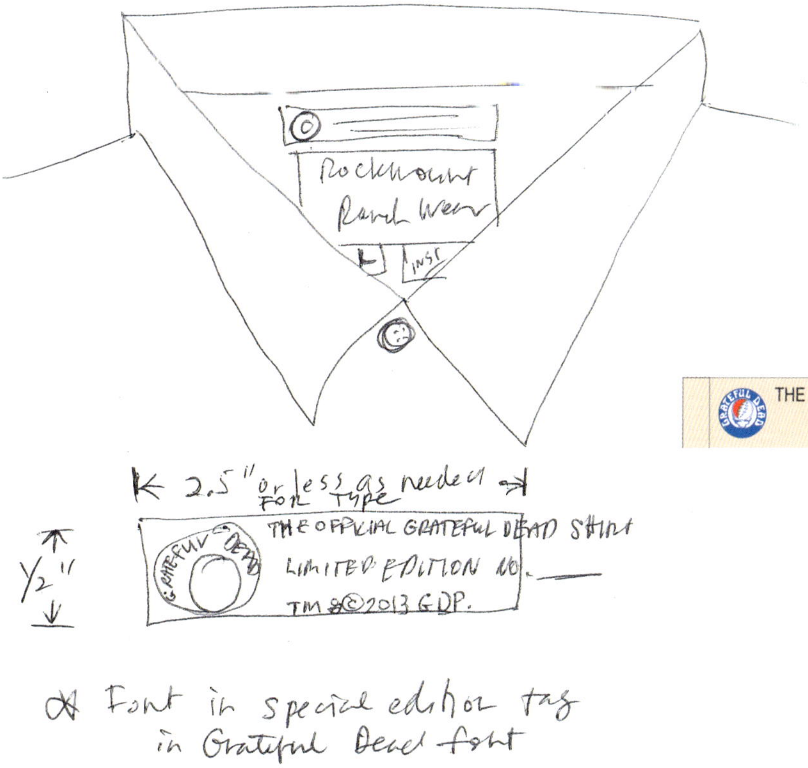

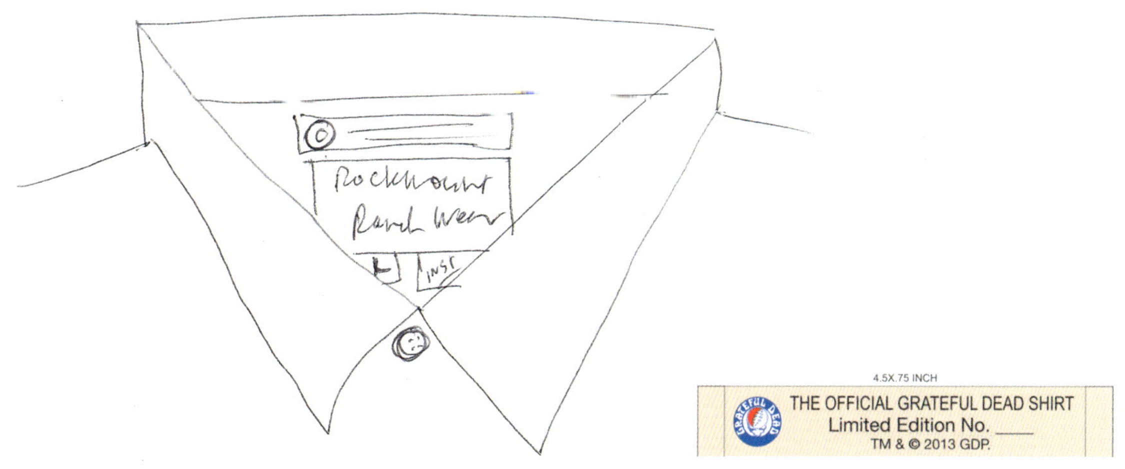
Rockmount
Ranch Wear
INST
4.5X.75 INCH
THE OFFICIAL GRATEFUL DEAD SHIRT
Limited Edition No. ____
TM & © 2013 GDP.
2.5" or less as needed for type
½"
GRATEFUL DEAD
THE OFFICIAL GRATEFUL DEAD SHIRT
LIMITED EDITION NO. ____
TM &© 2013 GDP.
Font in special edition tag
in Grateful Dead font

PHIL LESH & FRIENDS

We were invited to Red Rocks to meet Phil Lesh & Friends and attend their concert. This is a photo backstage with band member Larry Campbell in Rockmount. Jackie Greene (right) stays in touch, and we have seen him visit and perform numerous times in Denver and New Orleans.

LAWRENCE OF ANTARCTICA

This is one of those fun stories that comes out of nowhere and makes your day—maybe not so famous, but pretty funny.

Rockmount Reaches the Antarctic!

People go to the end of the world to get our shirts. We know our shirts are popular in a lot of places, but here is the first inquiry from the South Pole.

Subject: Good morning from Lawrence of Antarctica

Date: Sat, 12 Jun 2004

From: "Ahlin, Lawrence"

To: info@rockmount.com

I have a question for you—Can I buy some of your shirts and have them sent via mail? Currently I am stationed overseas so it would have to ship by USPS if I can order. Thanks for your time and response.

Lawrence Ahlin, Jr

McMurdo Station, Antarctica

Our reply:

Subject: Re: Good morning from Lawrence

Date: 6/11/2004

From: SWEIL

Reply To: Lawrence.Ahlin

Dear Lawrence,

We know the word is getting around but how did you hear about Rockmount?

What a treat to hear from Antarctica. My 6 year old will be thrilled. He has studied the poles (but has a preference for the north, something to do with Santa. . . .)

Anyway, we would be glad to receive your order but suggest you may prefer long sleeves. Also how about a report on what you do there!

How long does it take to receive something via USPS? I hope it is faster than here in Denver!

Give our regards to the penguins.

Steve Weil

rockmount.com

ALEX TURNER, ARCTIC MONKEYS

The rock band Arctic Monkeys seems like a logical choice to follow Antarctica. Alex Turner and the band wear Rockmount, as seen in many concert and album photos in Rockmount shirts and bolero jackets. They visited us in 2012 with their roadies and bus. Wazee, our yellow lab, is a fan, too.

ROBERT REDFORD

If he did nothing else but *Butch Cassidy and the Sundance Kid*, Robert Redford would forever be in the annals of American Western culture. But he did so much more, and Rockmount had a supporting role. Coincidentally, he was Jack Weil in *Havana*.

In 1996, we were first contacted by Sundance ski resort in Utah, saying that Mr. Redford wanted Rockmount to make the official shirt for the resort. When I asked what they had in mind, he put me in touch with the man who wanted it done. Redford chose the design details and colors that have been their consistent uniform for more than twenty-five years..

When *The Horse Whisperer* was filmed in 1998, the costume designer called us and said Redford asked her to order shirts for the cast from Rockmount. A feature in the *New York Times* showed him wearing a Rockmount plaid shirt from the movie. Over time, we saw him in many other Rockmount shirts.

One time, we heard from a lawyer without mandate, attempting to shake us down for having Redford's photos on our website. I said, "Ask Mr. Redford if he objects." We never heard back.

Well, they don't make 'em like Robert Redford anymore, but we have so much to remember him by.

Don Edwards Tie

We also had connections with Buck Brannaman, who was the inspiration of *The Horse Whisperer*. We have met Brannaman a few times, and he wears Rockmount. He is famous for his unique way of communicating with horses, creating a bond between horse and rider for best performance results.

Don Edwards (1939-2022), the cowboy singer, had a role in the movie. We produced a numbered, limited-edition silk scarf and tie in 2001 with him calf roping, based on the art of Joelle Smith.

MARTHA IN MARFA

Who has better taste than Martha Stewart?

In the art mecca of Marfa, Texas, a store called Among My Souvenirs (formerly Communitie Marfa) is owned by our friend of many years Kate Calder. Marfa is a cool, quirky, East Texas town known as an enclave for minimalist art, attracting an amazing array of artists and creative people—aka Rockmount country.

In the summer of 2024, Calder sold Rockmount shirts to Martha Stewart and her friend, photographer Douglas Friedman. Martha, the uber-arbiter of good taste, chose Rockmount vintage embroidery No. 6709 (left). Friedman was wearing Rockmount No. 6807.

TWO AND A HALF MEN (2003–2015)

Rockmount's Hollywood story includes television too.

Eddie Gorodetsky and Chuck Lorre have produced several hit TV comedies, including *Two and a Half Men* with Charlie Sheen. It turns out that Gorodetsky is a Rockmount fan. One day in 2012, Rockmount received a rush order for a bunch of shirts for the TV crew and cast. The Rockmount team jumped through hoops to get the order out within an hour so the shirts would be delivered in Burbank by 10 a.m. the next day. It's what we do when our customers have a special request. (One customer had recently asked us to draw a T-Rex on his package of Rockmount shirts. Done! Why? Who knows; but when you can do a little extra and make the customer happy, why not?) Helping the customer is what sets us apart from many online behemoths that don't have actual humans to personalize a customer's order. But, hey, we were fans of the show and figured if they like what we do, and we like what they do, there is something right in the world. But there is more to the story.

I mentioned to them that my family and I were traveling to Los Angeles later that week to attend a fabric show in the city. Luckily for us, we were invited to the filming at the Warner Brothers Studio in Burbank. We were picked up in a golf cart and taken to the set, where we watched the filming, met the crew and actors, and joined them for dinner.

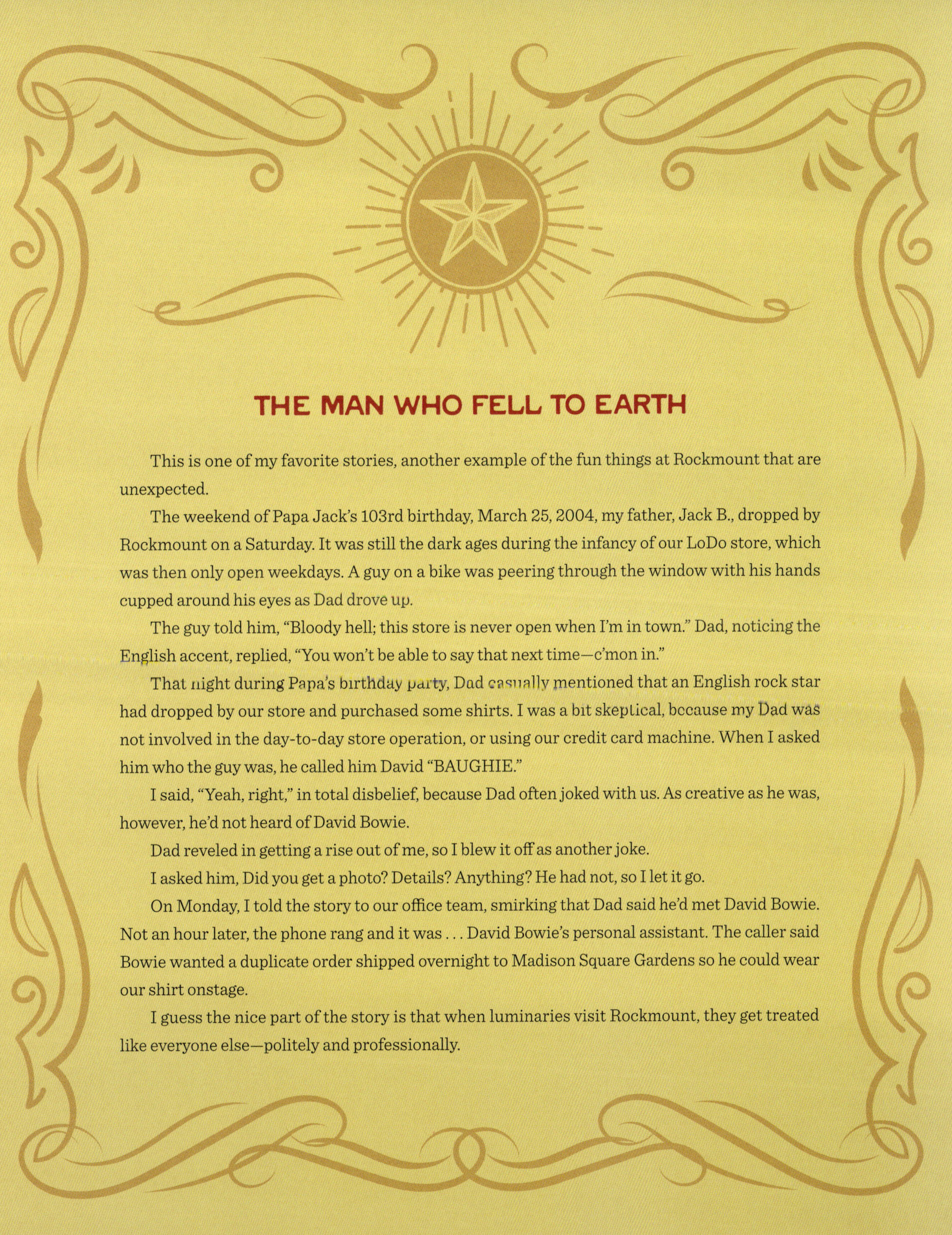

THE MAN WHO FELL TO EARTH

This is one of my favorite stories, another example of the fun things at Rockmount that are unexpected.

The weekend of Papa Jack's 103rd birthday, March 25, 2004, my father, Jack B., dropped by Rockmount on a Saturday. It was still the dark ages during the infancy of our LoDo store, which was then only open weekdays. A guy on a bike was peering through the window with his hands cupped around his eyes as Dad drove up.

The guy told him, "Bloody hell; this store is never open when I'm in town." Dad, noticing the English accent, replied, "You won't be able to say that next time—c'mon in."

That night during Papa's birthday party, Dad casually mentioned that an English rock star had dropped by our store and purchased some shirts. I was a bit skeptical, because my Dad was not involved in the day-to-day store operation, or using our credit card machine. When I asked him who the guy was, he called him David "BAUGHIE."

I said, "Yeah, right," in total disbelief, because Dad often joked with us. As creative as he was, however, he'd not heard of David Bowie.

Dad reveled in getting a rise out of me, so I blew it off as another joke.

I asked him, Did you get a photo? Details? Anything? He had not, so I let it go.

On Monday, I told the story to our office team, smirking that Dad said he'd met David Bowie. Not an hour later, the phone rang and it was . . . David Bowie's personal assistant. The caller said Bowie wanted a duplicate order shipped overnight to Madison Square Gardens so he could wear our shirt onstage.

I guess the nice part of the story is that when luminaries visit Rockmount, they get treated like everyone else—politely and professionally.

HANNAH MONTANA

The Denver Post
Parker: Cyrus Stylin' with Rockmount Shirt
By Penny Parker, Columnist
July 23, 2010

Miley Cyrus gave Denver-based Rockmount Ranch Wear some national television exposure.

Rockmount rocker.

LoDo-based Rockmount Ranch Wear got an unexpected shout-out from Miley Cyrus when her wildly popular show *Hannah Montana* premiered season four Tuesday night.

During the show, she gives a Rockmount shirt to her real-life dad Billy Ray Cyrus, who ends up wearing the glad rag. The design is shirt No. 6706, a black shirt with hand-embroidered red Hawaiian flowers.

The national TV exposure doesn't necessarily lead to higher shirt sales, but it helps spread buzz about the brand, Rockmount owner Steve Weil said.

"It reinforces our brand and reinforces our design direction," Weil said about the TV exposure. "It means a costume designer picked it up and bought it because (he or she) liked it."

This wasn't that shirt style's first TV time. William Shatner donned it during an episode of *Boston Legal*. "The beauty of it is it's so identifiable as our shirt," Weil said.

WILLIAM SHATNER AND JAMES SPADER

Go boldly where no man has gone before.

Oops, that's from another show. . . .

We know him best from *Star Trek,* when William Shatner commanded the *USS Enterprise* his way. James Spader masters eccentric roles, from *The Avengers, Sex, Lies and Videotape,* and *The Blacklist,* among many others.

William Shatner and James Spader in the 2008 *Boston Legal* episode "Happy Trails" both wear Rockmount. Shatner sports the same No. 6706 Paniolo Hibiscus embroidery shirt, but a different color from the one Billy Ray Cyrus wore in *Hannah Montana.*

Spader sports a two-tone vintage embroidery No. 6724.

LEFT: Shirt No. 6706-1 worn by William Shatner in a *Boston Legal* episode, except the flowers were white.

RIGHT: James Spader wore shirt No. 6724 in turquoise and brown in the same *Boston Legal* episode.

LATE NIGHT TV

We have stories from both *The Tonight Show* with Jay Leno and *Late Show* with David Letterman.

The *Late Show* did shows featuring top cities, including Denver. Rather than film from those actual places, however, they sent a crew to the cities to invite people from the cities to attend the show. This was before we had retail. Some of the crew were Rockmount fans and stopped by. They went into our sample room, and I asked them, "Please do not try on the samples." After they tried on everything and picked some shirts, they invited me, along with an entire studio audience, to travel to New York to attend the show the next day; they paid the flights and hotel. I took my buddy Gerry Engle (also Clapton trip)—one of the few people I know who can take off on a moment's notice. We met Rupert from Hello Deli (a recurring Letterman character). The Foo Fighters were the musical guests. We were front row, and it was so loud we could not hear the words. I became friends with one of the writers, John Bobey, and we get together from time to time. How could I not when he invited us to NYC as guests of the show?

After a flurry of news stories when Papa Jack celebrated his 107th birthday, *The Tonight Show* booking agents invited him to LA to be on the show as the world's oldest CEO. Unimpressed, Papa said no—airports had become such a hassle, and it was not worth it for a few minutes on TV.

I suggested to the show that they fly him privately, given his age. They said, "We don't fly Tom Cruise for interviews." I replied, "Tom Cruise is not 107 years old." So, the producers sent the comedian Mo Rocca to do the interview at Rockmount. I told the booker that they needed to treat Papa respectfully and not to make any jokes at his expense. They agreed.

So, Mo Rocca came with a crew to interview Papa. Mo has stopped by other times, too.

OPPOSITE: Mo Rocca at Rockmount, in No. 6851, bronc embroidered shirt.

Ranch
DENVER

TOM BRADY IN *GQ*

GQ Magazine featured seven-time Super Bowl quarterback Tom Brady in a cover story wearing Rockmount's signature shadow plaid No. 693 in 2005. We love that Rockmount is worn by all sorts of people, including athletes. We never pay to play—even in the Super Bowl. So, it's a nice surprise when we pop up in the media, especially worn by someone like Brady, who is an arbiter of fashion.

Apparently, one Tom Brady story is not enough.

This story surfaced from my friend Nick Forster, founder of the award-winning bluegrass band Hot Rize and also the founder and host of the syndicated radio program *eTown*:

> *A few years ago, my colleague Roger and I were early for a meeting in downtown Denver, so we decided to shop at Rockmount. Since Roger had never been to the store, I gave him a tour. It was a quiet morning with only two other shoppers in the store. We both tried on some shirts.*
>
> *I'm tall and thin, so hard to fit. I glanced across the room and saw another guy trying on*

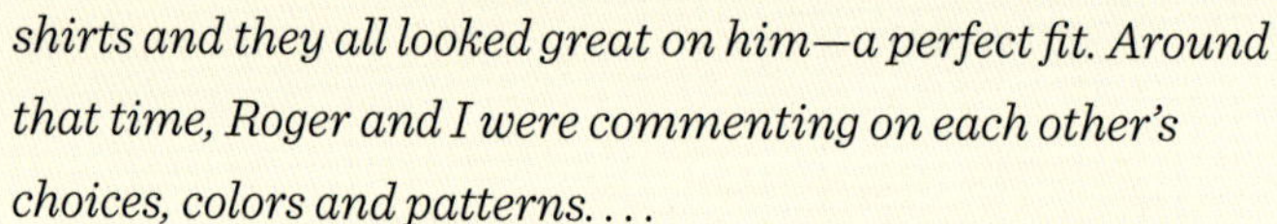

> *shirts and they all looked great on him—a perfect fit. Around that time, Roger and I were commenting on each other's choices, colors and patterns. . . .*

> *When Roger went into a changing room, a beautiful young woman came over and began pulling shirts off the Tall rack that she thought would work for me. I was happy to get the help and kind of amazed that she was paying attention to me, a total stranger. She helped me find shirts that I may not have chosen myself. I took a few into the changing room and then came out to show her, one at a time, which she then judged. She'd say, "No, not the right color," or "That one looks great, you've got to get it!"*
>
> *I thanked her and she walked away. Roger and I gathered up our shirts and headed to the cash register. The two other shoppers, the guy who looked great in every shirt and my beautiful shopping assistant, had already checked out. As we were paying, the woman at the cash register said, "Well, that was cool." I asked what she meant, and she said, "It's not every day that Tom Brady and Gisele Bündchen come here to shop."*

THE MEN'S FASHION BOOK

Rockmount Ranch Wear is included in *The Men's Fashion Book* (Phaidon, 2021). Years in the making, the book is considered the most comprehensive, global survey of 500 of the greatest contributors to men's fashion over two centuries. It brings together icons in the history of men's fashion with its brightest stars past, present, and future, including Cartier, Armani, Ferragamo, Ray-Ban, and Patek Philippe, among others.

Rockmount's inclusion in this definitive survey of world fashion is humbling because the Weil family has worked for three generations to create the brand as an end in itself. So, when the outside world recognizes our contribution to fashion, it validates our groundbreaking work and reputation.

Wendy and Steve Weil attended the book launch in New York City and met Jacob Gallagher, Men's Fashion Editor at the *Wall Street Journal*, who played a large part in producing the book. These photos are at the Phaidon book launch.

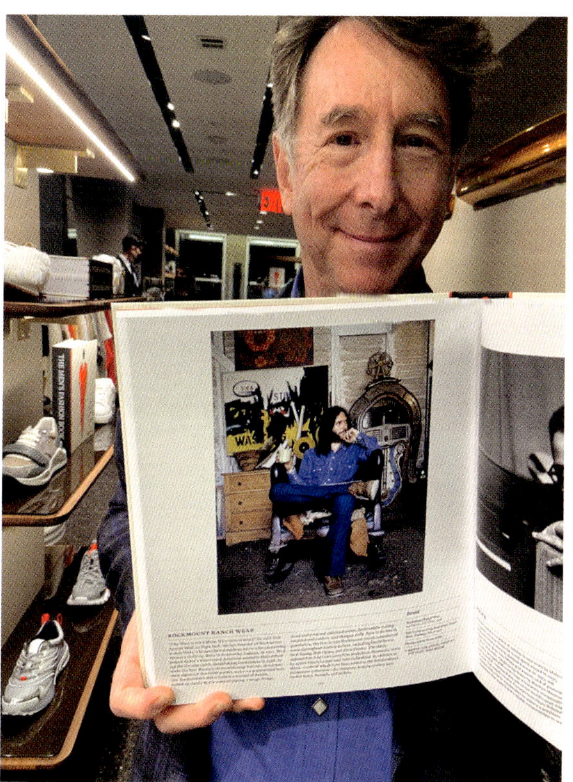

JOHN TRAVOLTA, *URBAN COWBOY*

The 1980 romantic country Western movie *Urban Cowboy* marked the first time that the Western genre went Main Street, first nationally and then internationally, where it has remained in fashion ever since.

My father, Jack B. Weil, designed two shirts worn by John Travolta in that film—No. 678, a solid jade-green cotton blend with white piping (seen in red on the left catalog page), and No. 6199, a red satin with white piping and hidden pockets (as in the top right catalog image).

ROCKMOUNT CUSTOM FITTED SOLID SHIRTS

(top left) **Royal men's shirt:** High Count U.S. 65% poly/35% cotton that wears long and hard. Expertly sewn with curved yokes.
Light colors: white, natural, yellow, light blue, mint. Sizes 14-18. Style 650 $29.75 (add $1.00 17½, 18)
Medium colors: royal, navy, brown, black, lavender, rust, pink, kelly. Sizes 14-18. Style 677 $30.50

(top right) **Men's & Women's Saddle Stitch:** Ours alone, this Rockmount design has been popular for generations. Special contrast stitching, 65% poly/35% cotton. **Men's Colors: navy, red, brown, black, white. Sizes: 14-18 Style 6801 $31.75** (add $1.00 17½, 18)

Women's colors: navy, red, brown. Sizes: 30-40. Style 7801 $31.00

(bottom right) **Solid, Scallop Stitch:** Special Rockmount embroidery on collar, pockets and yokes, 65% poly/35% cotton. **Colors: white, lavender, peach, pink, yellow, mint, light blue. Sizes: 14½-18.**
Style 670 $31.50 (add $1.00 17½, 18)

Solid, piping: Contrast piping on yokes, pockets and special cuffs, richly dyed U.S. 65% poly/35% cotton. **Colors: burgundy, camel, jade, purple. Sizes 14½-18. Style 678 $35.00** (add $1.00 17½, 18)

(bottom left) **Men's & Women's Solids:** more popular than ever, this best seller is durable, has Rockmount's custom fit, 65% poly/35% cotton. Men's have diamond snaps, women's round. Matching shirt for children. **Men's colors: turquoise, red, black, gold. Sizes: 14-18. Style 640 $31.50** (add $1.00 17½, 18)

Women's colors: gold, turquoise, red, white, black Sizes: 30-40. Style 740 $28.75

Children's Colors: gold, turquoise, red, white, black Sizes: 2-6. Style 840(B) $20.50 Sizes 8-16. Style 840(Y) $21.75

-3-

Men's blue & black satin shirts: Bes selling western satin, Rockmount's classic with piping is washable. Features hidder pockets. Companion shirt for women. **Colors: royal, red, black with white piping, and white with black piping Sizes: 14-18.**
Style 6199 $33.50 (add $1.00 17½ 18)

His felt hat: Rockmount's special fur blend in Cattleman crease. **Colors: Sil verbelly 60, Black 62, Sorrel 66 $36.0**

Women's blue Satin with fringe: Al ways a Rockmount favorite, washabl Satin with looped fringe that will neve ravel. Companion shirt for men, se cover. **Colors: royal, red, natural, rust Sizes: 30-40.**
Style 7198 $33.80

Her felt hat: Rockmount's fur-blend i RCA crease. **Colors: White 81 $38.50 Silverbelly 70, Black 72, Sorrel 76 Brown 79 $36.00**
Also same style in 100% wool Sizes: 6⅝-7½ Style 1750 Now $12.95!

Women's white Satin: Rockmount's spe cial washable satin, with piping. Matche men's above. **Colors: white, black, re Sizes: 30-40. Style 7199 $31.50**

ROCKMOUNT CELEBRITY SHIRTS

(left) **Platinum Grey men's shirt:** This dress shirt has a fine woven diamond pattern. It will always stay neat, permanent press 80% poly/20% cotton. **Colors: Platinum Grey, Turquoise. Sizes: 14-18. Style 623 $30.95** (add $1.00 17½, 18)

His felt hat: Rockmount's premium fur-blend in Cattleman's crease. **Colors: Silverbelly 60, Black 62, Sorrel 66 $36.00**

Matching Women's Turquoise shirt: Features self-ruffle on collar, front and back yokes, and cuffs. The crisp cotton/poly blend has a small diamond weave that stays neat. Comes with ribbon tie. **Colors: Platinum Grey, Turquoise. Sizes: 30-40. Style 723 $33.50**

(above) **Men's & Women's black/red fringe shirt** Look your best in this striking combination. See t beautiful curve of the yokes, a Rockmount trad mark. The front and back yokes are trimmed wi fringe and piping, and sleeves have fringe to cuffs. O special looped fringe will never ravel. The fabric 65% poly/35% cotton. Men's has hidden pock **Men's sizes: 14-18. Style 6627 $41.95** (add $1. 17½, 18)

Women's sizes: 30-40. Style 7627 $38.00

Her black felt hat: RCA crease Rockmount fu blend for men and women. **Colors: Black 72, Silve belly 70, Sorrel 76, Dark Brown 79 $36.00 Al same style in 100% wool. Style 1750 now $12.95**

-6-

Rockmount catalog, 1987. Steve directed photography and layout.

In the ’80s, Western fashion and culture blew up in popular culture for the first time because of this film’s ubiquitous, popularizing social effect.

The shirts were likely bought by the studio at a Western store in Los Angeles, as this was before the time that films began contacting us directly, about 2000, with the advent of the internet. The Web was a game changer in terms of access. Prior to this film, other early films with Rockmount clothing included *The Misfits* (1961) with Clark Gable and Marilyn Monroe, and *Love Me Tender* (1956), starring Elvis Presley. However, no other earlier film had the kind of massive social impact of *Urban Cowboy*.

With fame comes hardships. The entire US Western apparel industry expanded fast and furiously due to this movie introducing the urban cowboy fashion fad, seemingly an overnight success. Seeing growth, most companies committed resources, hired workers, increased production, built more factories, and produced inventory to meet the business spike. Hundreds of new Western stores suddenly opened across the US and around the world. Everyone was blinded by the bright lights, believing it would go on forever.

However, the industry forgot a fundamental: business is cyclical; every boom has its bust. This was no exception, as if someone turned off the faucet as fast as they had turn it on. Everyone had enough trendy hats, shirts, and boots. Demand dried up. Inventories burgeoned, brands big and small went bankrupt, and many new stores closed. Rockmount went from having inventory last in stock for only days to having excessive stock that took years to sell. Still, my father and grandfather were good businessmen and were not buried by the overnight shutdown when the fad cooled in a satiated market. We did not bet the ranch but had the experience and resources to endure the worst business decline in both our company’s and the industry’s history.

This was the scenario when I arrived at Rockmount in 1981, having finished graduate school, just in time to see the gold rush become a fire sale. One of life’s great lessons, if you’re lucky, is to endure a downturn and help guide a turnaround. My big takeaway is that the *Urban Cowboy* fad was garish and costumey. My challenge, some years later, was to create fashion for a lifestyle, not a fad. I concentrated on making shirts my friends would wear and make them a lasting part of popular culture.

BOB DYLAN

While I was growing up, Bob Dylan was my favorite artist. Over the years, we have seen him wear many Rockmount shirts at concerts, events, and on album covers. The first time I saw him in a Rockmount shirt was when he wore a pink gabardine from my earliest vintage collection in the early 1990s. The shirt is actually based on a women's sleeveless design with very stylized mirrored pockets and saddle stitching; it's one of my favorite designs done in the 1950s by my father. This kind of special treatment helped create the Western identity. I reinterpreted the design for men in long sleeve, but true to the past, in rayon gabardine. Dylan wore this shirt in New Orleans, and it appeared on the *Love and Theft* album cover and posters, 2001. Dylan wore it for years. We reintroduced it a second time when his album came out then. He bought the shirt in New York City at Billy Martin's Western Wear, which was instrumental in raising the bar and building a market for high-end Western wear; sadly, the store is now closed.

Imagine my thrill when I first saw Dylan wearing Rockmount, combined with my love for his music.

Later he wore our white sawtooth signature design No. 6940 with black diamond snaps when then-US President Obama awarded him the Presidential Medal of Freedom in 2012.

Dylan shops at Rockmount's LoDo flagship store. One time, in 2007, he bought seventeen shirts. My good friend Gretchen Bunn helped him while he was shopping, and she mentioned we had his photos on the wall. He said he knew, because he had seen them on earlier visits. (He had slipped in undetected.) This time, he was very inconspicuous too, wearing shades and a wool cap.

As a lifelong Dylan fan, I can think of no better accolade than seeing this creative visionary wearing Rockmount.

ABOVE: Courtesy of Billy Martin's store, New York.

LEFT: President Barack Obama awarding Bob Dylan the Medal of Freedom, 2012. Courtesy of the Barack Obama Presidential Library and the National Library.

OPPOSITE: No. 6940 is the shirt Dylan wore at the award ceremony.

BOB DYLAN, MARK KNOPFLER AND DIRE STRAITS

In 2012 Wendy took me to the first night of two Denver concerts, with Mark Knopfler opening for Bob Dylan. We attended the concert the first night. The next day, who should walk into Rockmount but Knopfler and bandmates Richard Bennett (guitar) and Guy Fletcher (keyboard). They said they would wear their new shirts at the second show. We saw pictures of Bennett in his Rockmount denim shirt No. 640-DT onstage. This is one of the unexpected pleasures at Rockmount—not knowing who is going to drop by unexpectedly.

Good shirts sing.

JACK WHITE, THE WHITE STRIPES

Acclaimed musician Jack White has visited Rockmount a few times and invited us to his shows. Once, in 2009, a friend from England walked in at the same time as Jack, and I had to decide which way to turn. Of course I chose Fiona, but Jack invited us to his concert anyway. The music was loud, and I kept thinking the peeling paint at the Ogden Theater would erupt into fire!

When the Foothills Art Center exhibit *Cowboys & Rock Stars* was staged, Jack lent us his Rockmount red fringe shirt No. 6723 with matching pants for the rock star section, which also featured Bob Dylan, Eric Clapton, and Paul McCartney. The 2010 exhibit chronicled Rockmount's seven decades impact through our archive of fashion, memorabilia, and advertising.

JAKOB DYLAN

Bob Dylan's son Jakob Dylan is part of the Wallflowers. They played Red Rocks in 2024 and visited Rockmount while in Denver.

Like father, like son.

OPPOSITE: Left to right: Mark Knopfler, me, Richard Bennett, and Guy Fletcher.

ABOVE: Jack White's red shirt and pants.

LEFT: Jakob Dylan with Rockmount's Kristie Ann Dischler, 2024.

VINCE VAUGHN

Actor and comedian Vince Vaughn visited Denver to attend a hockey game in 2010 and popped into Rockmount. He found a kid's shirt he liked and insisted repeatedly that we come up with the same design in his size, and he's a big guy. Catching on to his shtick, I suggested he buy two or three kid-sized shirts and snap them together (never mind the extra sleeves). He thought better of it and found one his size.100

Vaughn has worn Rockmount in movies, including a denim embroidery No. 6783-DEN in the 2020 crime thriller *Arkansas*.

WESLEY SCHULTZ, THE LUMINEERS

Wes Schultz, lead singer in the folk-rock band The Lumineers, visited Rockmount ahead of their 2024 European tour. We love their latest album, *Brightside*. The Schultz and Weil families are neighbors, so it was fun showing them around Rockmount while the new album played. Brandy Schultz took these pictures of me. The last time a rock star's wife took pics of me was with Eric Clapton! Wes is wearing our No. 6100 fleece shirt.

Wes Schultz, Steve Weil, and Humboldt (head of security). Photo by Brandy Schultz.

BILL PULLMAN

Actor Bill Pullman was in Denver for the 2017 Denver International Film Festival and visited Rockmount. He picked up a number of shirts. We have photos with him at Rockmount and with our friend John Hickenlooper, then Denver mayor. Pullman was cordial and invited us to his screening.

TONY CURTIS

Tony Curtis visited Denver in 1996 to attend the annual Denver International Film Festival. We met at a party, and he was interested that I was in the Western wear business.

The next morning the phone rang, and it was Curtis asking for me. Thinking it was a joke, I picked up the phone and made an off-hand comment, "Who IS this?"

Undeterred, he said he would like to come by Rockmount and asked how long it would take to get a cab from the Warwick Hotel to Rockmount. I told him I'd pick him up in a few minutes.

This was years before we opened our downtown retail store. This photo shows us together in our old sample room. Curtis bought a hat and a shirt. Meanwhile, Dad, Papa, and I chatted with him. We had some laughs, and he hung around long enough to go to lunch with us at the Denver Athletic Club.

He was a colorful and charming guy who seemed to have few, if any, pretensions.

Tony Curtis visits the Weils at Rockmount, 1996.

JEREMY SWIFT (*TED LASSO*) AND NATALIE GOLD (*SUCCESSION*)

Our friend Sheryl Globus co-wrote and directed the road trip film *Welcome to the Fishbowl,* with Donald Rae, which features a shopping segment at Rockmount's historic downtown headquarters.

We met *Ted Lasso* star Jeremy Swift prior to the filming when he did a script reading, and he dropped by Rockmount to shop. I had just seen the *Ted Lasso* episode with him playing the Higgins role during the scene when the team burns precious items from each member to overcome a streak of bad luck. Higgins burned his cat Cindy Clawford's collar. When I mentioned I loved that scene, Swift told me he ad-libbed that line.

Later, when Natalie Gold and he were filming at Rockmount over two days, we hung out a bit and ate lunch together. Gold talked about *Succession* and mentioned she was friends with the actress Justine Lupe. She knew that Justine was from Denver and had attended the Denver School of the Arts (as did my son). I had just seen the series *Nobody Wants This*, where Justine plays a central part completely different from her previous role in *Succession*.

The crew had over fifty people running around with set and design, sound, lighting, makeup, you name it. Rockmount stayed open during the entire time, though the sidewalk was sometimes blocked and we kept the background noise down. They invited us to the wrap party, capping a very fun experience overall.

Natalie Gold and Jeremy Swift with Steve Weil at Rockmount during filming, 2024.

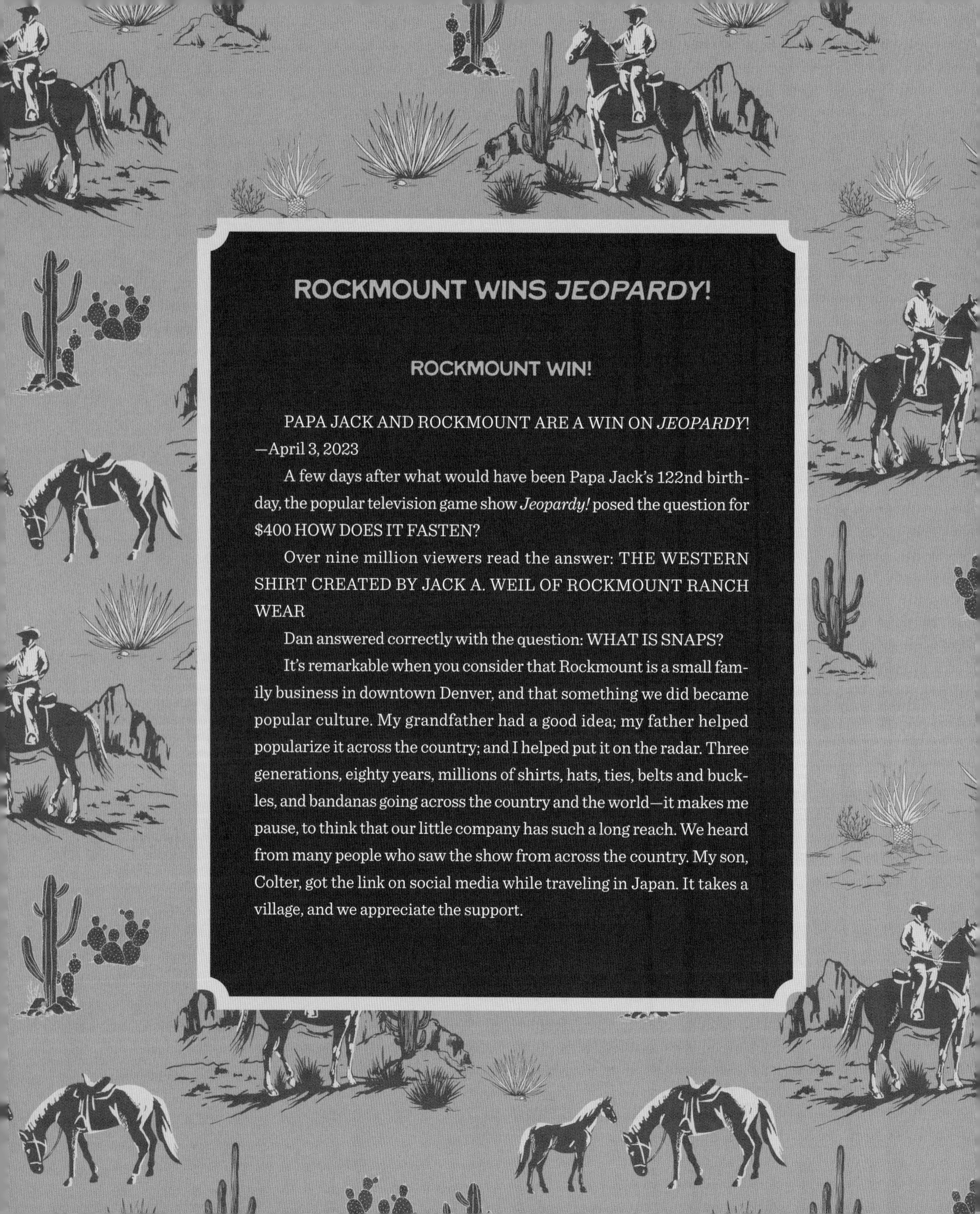

ROCKMOUNT WINS *JEOPARDY*!

ROCKMOUNT WIN!

PAPA JACK AND ROCKMOUNT ARE A WIN ON *JEOPARDY*!
—April 3, 2023

A few days after what would have been Papa Jack's 122nd birthday, the popular television game show *Jeopardy!* posed the question for $400 HOW DOES IT FASTEN?

Over nine million viewers read the answer: THE WESTERN SHIRT CREATED BY JACK A. WEIL OF ROCKMOUNT RANCH WEAR

Dan answered correctly with the question: WHAT IS SNAPS?

It's remarkable when you consider that Rockmount is a small family business in downtown Denver, and that something we did became popular culture. My grandfather had a good idea; my father helped popularize it across the country; and I helped put it on the radar. Three generations, eighty years, millions of shirts, hats, ties, belts and buckles, and bandanas going across the country and the world—it makes me pause, to think that our little company has such a long reach. We heard from many people who saw the show from across the country. My son, Colter, got the link on social media while traveling in Japan. It takes a village, and we appreciate the support.

BRIAN SETZER

Guitarist Brian Setzer blends doo-wop, hip-hop, and rockabilly with big-band swing. His band and he wear Rockmount. They all wear our bolero jacket No. 1110. The *Guitar Player* magazine cover is from 2010, and the band photo is from 2018, sent by the band.

WOODY HARRELSON

Woody Harrelson and Kiefer Sutherland star in the movie *The Cowboy Way,* 1994. Harrelson is wearing Rockmount's long-running signature classic No. 640 with sawtooth pockets and diamond snaps. Universal Pictures kindly sent us this promotional studio photo after we supplied the shirts.

Woody Harrelson in *The Cowboy Way* movie, wearing No. 640 shirt. Courtesy of Universal Pictures.

GENE SIMMONS, KISS

Back in the dark ages of 2003, Rockmount got a KISS from the band's flashy front man, Gene Simmons. Gene stopped by Rockmount with Audra Lynn, *Playboy's* "Miss October" centerfold that year.

Simmons purchased two shirts: our custom black Plonge leather No. 6666 and the signature stonewashed denim No. 640-DS. Audra left with shirts in tight-fitting leopard velour and white eyelet. Simmons has been seen wearing our shirts many times, as picked up in the media.

RIGHT: This photo of Simmons and Steve was in Rockmount's old sample room before we opened the retail store.

ROBERT TAYLOR, LOU DIAMOND PHILLIPS, BAILEY CHASE AND *LONGMIRE*

Many *Longmire* characters in the modern-day Western taking place in Wyoming wore Rockmount in many of its sixty-three episodes throughout its run, until 2017. Robert Taylor plays the title role, Sheriff Walt Longmire, an iconic lone hero. He wore many Rockmount shirts, including denim No. 640-DS. Lou Diamond Phillips plays Henry Standing Bear and wore a number of shirts, including our plaids No. 621 red, No. 694 plaid, and our fleece No. 6100. Bailey Chase played Deputy Branch Connally and wore our denim shirt.

Craig Johnson, our friend of many years, wrote *The Longmire Mysteries* upon which the modern Western TV series is based. We were honored to be asked to supply wardrobe to the show, which filmed six seasons and continues to be broadcast on Paramount+. Craig and his wife, Judy, operate the Bucking Buffalo Supply Co. in Buffalo, Wyoming, where they have carried Rockmount since 1995.

LEFT: Rockmount red plaid No. 621 similar as worn by Lou Diamond Phillips.

RIGHT: Robert Anderson wearing Rockmount No. 640-DS. Courtesy Longmire/Garson Studios.

DENNIS QUAID

Dennis Quaid and Meg Ryan both star in the movie *Flesh and Bone* (1993). Quaid wears two Rockmount shirts in the film: a solid white with single point pocket and our signature blue shadow plaid No. 693. The white shirt is featured here because there is a scene when Meg wears his shirt. Apparently wearing Rockmount is good for the soul, because they were married after the movie was filmed.

As for the Rockmount shadow plaid, one of our most popular designs, we have images of it on many A-listers, including Ben Affleck on the street and Al Pacino and Robin Williams in the movie *Insomnia* (2002). Additionally, it is worn by musicians Don Henley, Garth Brooks, and Blake Shelton, among others.

LEFT: Rockmount's shadow plaid, one of our most popular designs, has been worn by a wide range of A-listers.

OPPOSITE: Paramount Pictures kindly sent us these promotional studio photos of Dennis Quaid, Meg Ryan, and James Caan after we supplied the shirts.

RICK NIELSEN, CHEAP TRICK

Normally, we think of being fans of rock stars, but once in a while, they become our fans. Rick Nielsen, lead guitarist and primary songwriter of Cheap Trick, has invited us to Red Rocks a number of times as his guest. He has sent us photos wearing his Rockmount with Henry Kissinger, Pete Townsend, Queen, Sir George Martin (in Rockmount vintage 2-tone embroidery), and Morley Safer.

He wears a range of Rockmount in the photos including our Hawaiian floral embroidery No. 6706, and black fringe shirt No. 6723.

Rick Nielsen sent us these photos:

TOP LEFT: Rick Nielsen in Rockmount vintage floral embroidery with Jay Leno

SECOND LEFT: Sir George Martin (managed the Beatles) in Rockmount vintage 2-tone floral embroidery with Rick Nielsen

THIRD LEFT: Morley Safer (*60 Minutes*) and Rick Nielsen in Rockmount vintage Paniolo Hibiscus embroidery

BOTTOM LEFT: Pete Townsend with Rick Nielsen in Rockmount vintage Paniolo Hibiscus embroidery

ABOVE: Queen with Rick Nielsen in Rockmount No. 6723 vintage fringe shirt.

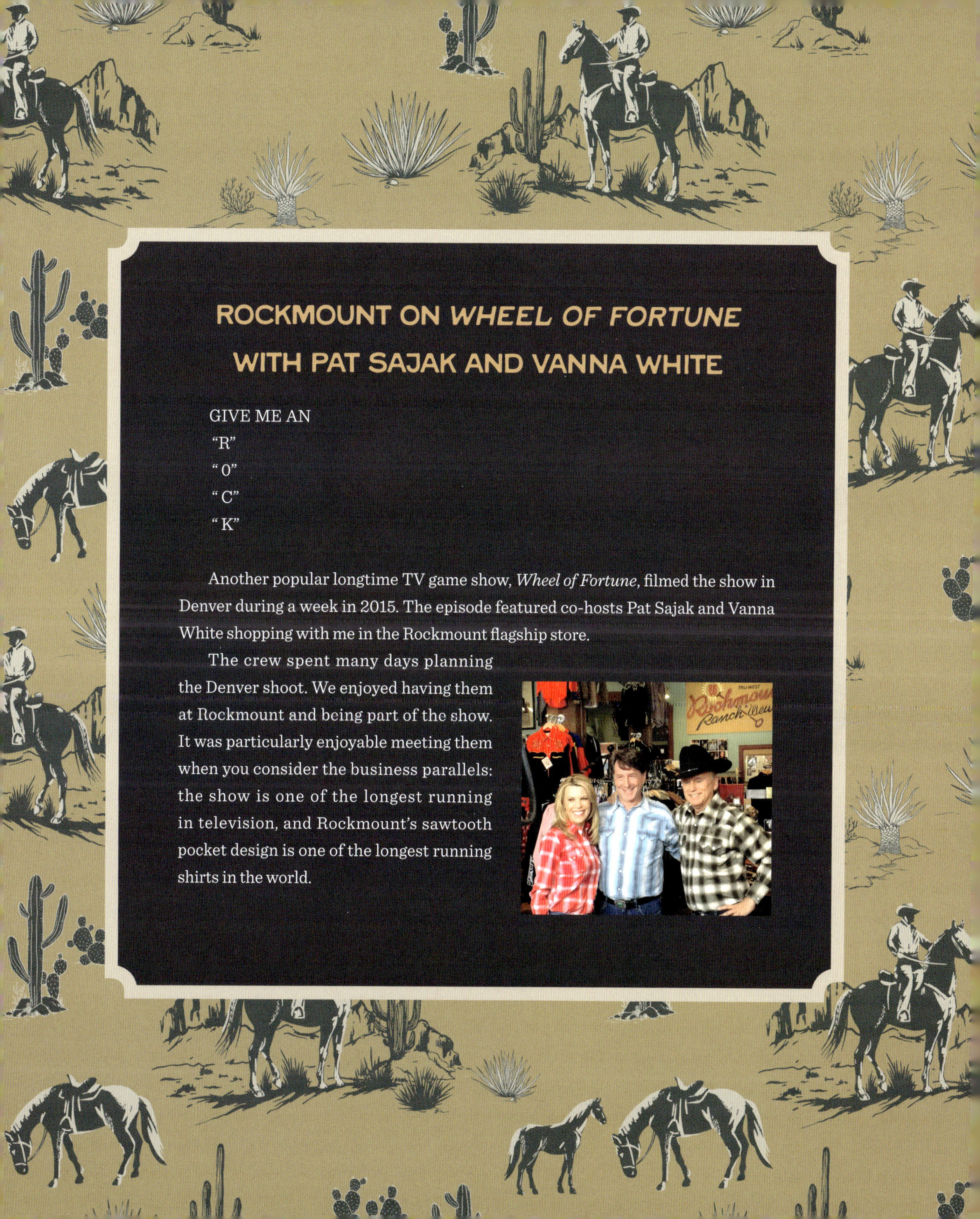

ROCKMOUNT ON *WHEEL OF FORTUNE* WITH PAT SAJAK AND VANNA WHITE

GIVE ME AN
"R"
" 0"
" C"
" K"

Another popular longtime TV game show, *Wheel of Fortune*, filmed the show in Denver during a week in 2015. The episode featured co-hosts Pat Sajak and Vanna White shopping with me in the Rockmount flagship store.

The crew spent many days planning the Denver shoot. We enjoyed having them at Rockmount and being part of the show. It was particularly enjoyable meeting them when you consider the business parallels: the show is one of the longest running in television, and Rockmount's sawtooth pocket design is one of the longest running shirts in the world.

BONNIE RAITT AND JAMES "HUTCH" HUTCHINSON

Musical artists Bonnie Raitt and James "Hutch" Hutchinson have played together much of their careers. Hutch is a bass player. He visits us at Rockmount when they play Denver. Hutch carries various Rockmounts in his stage wardrobe. We have photos of him in plaids and our hops embroidery No. 6799-BEER. One of the earlier visits was in November 2005. They invited us to the concert, which coincidentally was Bonnie's 56th birthday. We joined her backstage for cake.

Penny Parker, columnist, the *Rocky Mountain News* reported:

IT RATES WITH RAITT: Rockmount Ranch Wear heir Steve Weil had his cake and ate it too after the rockin' Raitt concert.

The wily Weil wrangled an invite to the post-concert backstage birthday party from James "Hutch" Hutchinson, the band's bass guitarist, who spent a bundle on a bundle of shirts at the LoDo western wear shop.

When Weil learned it was Raitt's birthday, he sent the singer a pink "girlie T-shirt" with a Rockmount logo designed by Jack A. Weil in the '40s.

Raitt was fighting a cold so she skipped the shopping trip.

"Hutch called and said she really liked it and she wanted to meet us after the show," said Weil, who was treated to VIP seats by the band. "They were so nice to us, I was very touched."

Hutch stays in touch. He wrote when he did a benefit concert during the pandemic wearing Rockmount:

The Weight with Ringo and Robbie Robertson—Playing for Change—Song Around the World in Rockmount.

I watched the link he sent and saw Hutch wearing Rockmount's red shadow plaid No. 693.

Another time he wrote:

From Hutch Hutchinson, longtime bass player with Bonnie Raitt to Steve Weil at Rockmount

Saw and hung with The Who in Vegas on Friday, the night before our first Stones show. Stones show went great. Bonnie and band had the audience on their feet from the very first tune! Wore one of your shirts and had compliments all down the line. Keith (Richards) went OOOOOH!!! Black with Flowers! Shades of Gram Parsons! He said that I out-cowboy'd Bobby Keys. Who is originally from New Mexico! Great seein' you last week.

All the best,

HUTCH

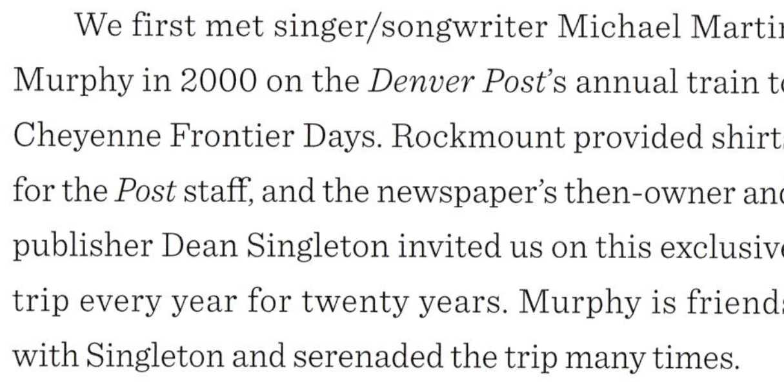

MICHAEL MARTIN MURPHY

We first met singer/songwriter Michael Martin Murphy in 2000 on the *Denver Post*'s annual train to Cheyenne Frontier Days. Rockmount provided shirts for the *Post* staff, and the newspaper's then-owner and publisher Dean Singleton invited us on this exclusive trip every year for twenty years. Murphy is friends with Singleton and serenaded the trip many times.

Michael is based in Colorado and often tours around the state. I asked him to model for our catalog in 2000, which he did in Colorado Springs, ahead of playing a concert there. He is a true gentleman, and hanging out with him is a lot of fun.

Michael Martin Murphy wears No. 640-DS (above) and onstage shadow plaid No. 693 (left) for the Rockmount catalog.

DON HENLEY

Rocker Don Henley, a founding member of The Eagles and solo performer after they broke up, has been seen in many Rockmount shirts over the years. A friend of his came into Rockmount and told me that Henley has a copy of my *Western Shirts* book on his coffee table. We have many concert photos of him wearing our signature shadow plaid No. 693 in various colors, including blue, red, and brown. Here he is wearing a vintage variation with horseshoe applique, which I reintroduced based on a '50s design by Jack B.

This photo from an Aspen concert was sent to us in 2003 by a fan in attendance.

JOHN DENVER COLLECTION

Our good friend Chris Tetzeli, a concert promoter in Denver, runs 7S Management, representing some very fine artists and the John Denver Estate. John Denver (1947–97) epitomized the Western vibe in his music and wore Rockmount. Tetzeli asked us to collaborate on a collection based on some of the late singer's shirts. We produced a numbered, limited-edition collection of six shirts in 2015, which sold out fast.

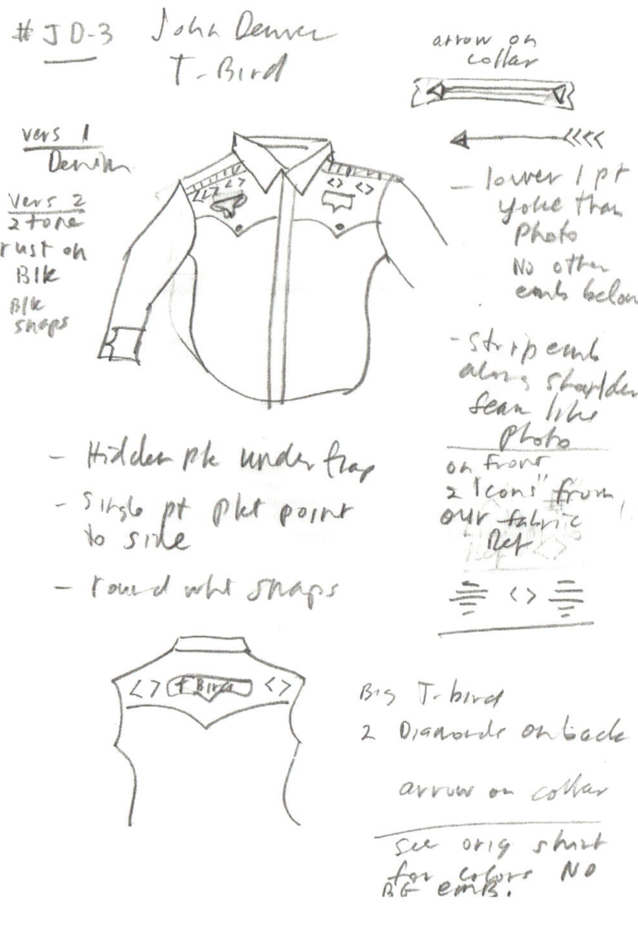

These are from the John Denver shirt collection, including the design artwork and limited-edition label.

THIS PAGE AND FACING: These mountain and floral shirt designs pick up on John Denver's *Rocky Mountain High* theme.

GRETSCH AND MARTIN GUITARS

Rockmount collaborates with various leading guitar companies on shirt collections, including Gretsch and Martin.

The Gretsch shirt project was a partnership with Terry Dennis from Evercast, who does marketing for musical artists and brands. The shirts sold very well over a number of years and were released again in 2025.

Chris Martin worked with us on custom shirts too. Martin, like Rockmount, is a family business, but theirs dates to 1833!

BILLY STRINGS

Billy Strings and his band wear Rockmount. They are all wearing matching 6724 two-tone Rockmount vintage embroideries on the *Jimmy Kimmel Live!* show.

THE KILLERS

It's not every day an entire band and their bus show up at Rockmount. (Humboldt is the yellow Labrador, our head of security.) It's lucky our loading area is big enough for a bus! The Killers were in town to play at Red Rocks. They shopped and invited us to the concert. A good day.

ROY ROGERS

The "King of the Cowboys" had a huge role in popularizing the Western lifestyle in both film and music. His family collaborated with us in 2001 on numbered, limited-edition Happy Trails silk ties and scarves. We also made socks with the Roy Rogers motif.

"KING OF THE COWBOYS"
ROY ROGERS
TRIGGER
Many Happy Trails
Roy Rogers
& Trigger
Roy Rogers
KING OF THE COWBOYS
Roy Rogers
KING OF THE COWBOYS
RR
RR
ROY ROGERS
"KING OF THE
COWBOYS"

OTIS TAYLOR

The renowned blues banjo player Otis Taylor is a longtime friend from Boulder, Colorado. We love hearing him in concert and have attended many of his performances, including New York City and Denver.

Taylor has an interesting history from his days chasing vintage Native American jewelry and more. He has made many visits to Rockmount and asked us to do a shirt collaboration in 2013. The shirt featured Santa Cruz guitars. Here is a clipping of Taylor wearing our signature art deco design No. 6705 from the *Rocky Mountain News*. Also, this is a drawing of the shirt we designed together and a photo of the finished product.

6 SPOTLIGHT ROCKY

cover story

ELLEN JASKOL/ROCKY MOUNTAIN NEWS

Otis Taylor became an antiques dealer during a hiatus from music that lasted almost 20 years. He's shown at his home in Boulder with paintings by his father and part of his collection of antique banjos and other instruments. At left is a ball of old shoestrings he got from a Denver shoeshiner.

Blues pull Taylor back

In this clipping from the *Rocky Mountain News*, Taylor is wearing our signature art deco design No. 6705.

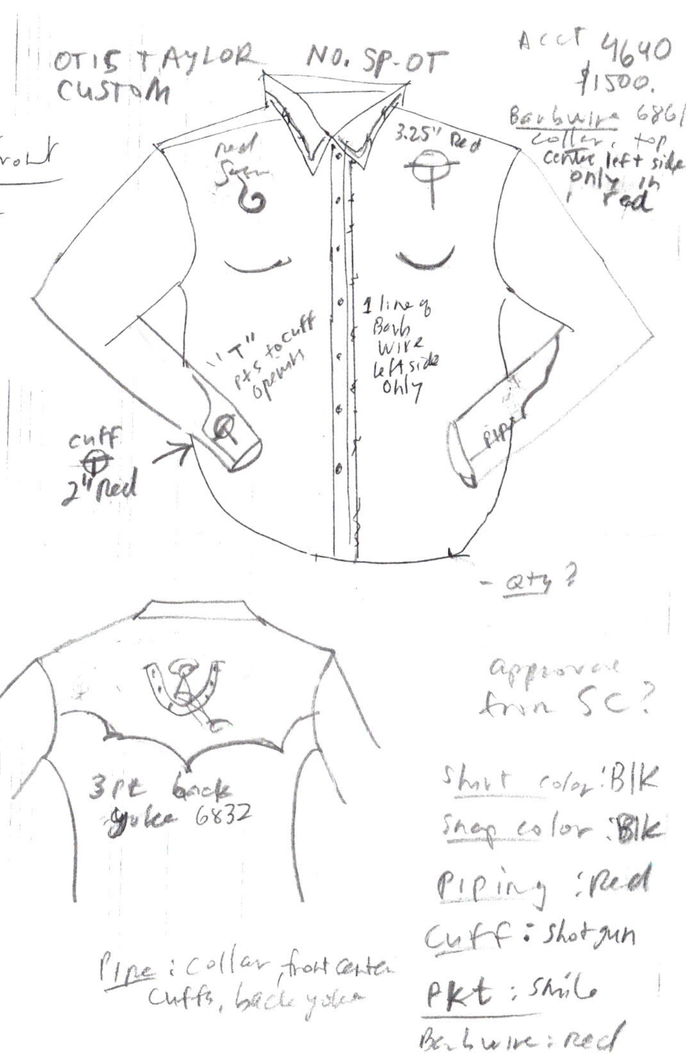

This is a drawing of the shirt we designed together

. . . and this is the finished product.

Years ago, Otis called me when his wife saw we had Civil War caps online. I told him we'd made them for many years for both North and South reenactment battles held on battlefields with historical significance. Many were sold to reenactors in Europe too. Both the Union blue and Confederate gray hats were always sold together. He was okay with my explanation, but his concern stuck with me. But, after a white supremacist murdered nine worshippers at a historic African American church in Charleston, South Carolina, in 2015, Rockmount dropped the caps. While I feel strongly that history must be viewed in context and that there is value in dialogue, the last thing I want to do is perpetuate hatred or racial bias.

SAM SMITH

We first met Sam Smith when he visited Rockmount in 2015. The British rocker and his entourage visit Rockmount whenever he plays in Denver. They hang out and shop for shirts, hats, and more before their concerts. Smith invited us to the concerts at Ball Arena (home of the Denver Nuggets, Colorado Avalanche, and Colorado Mammoth). In fact, while shopping at Rockmount on his first visit, Smith posted on his Instagram account with over 14 MILLION followers—not bad publicity for our small, family-owned Western wear business. As we always say, you never know how the day will end at Rockmount!

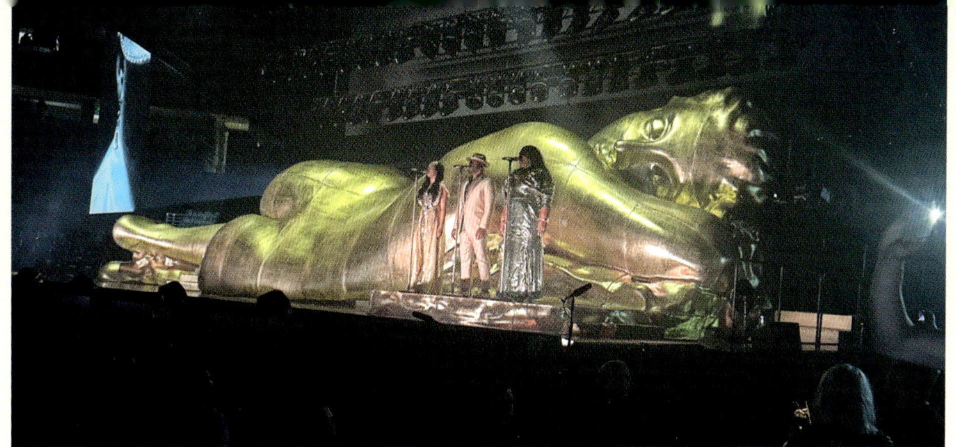

The concert photos are from 2025. The gold reclining figure must have been 75 feet long!

FRETLIGHT
Chris Isaak
Rock On!
GAS
CHRIS ISAAK
WENDY
STEVE
THANKS!
Chris Isaak
LIVE AT THE FILLMORE
2010
VIP
I love snap shirts. I always stop at
Rockmount Ranch Wear when I'm in Denver and
end up buying a bunch of cowboy shirts. I
guess my taste in shirts has been the same
since I was a kid.
– Chris Isaac
OUR PRESIDENT ROOSEVELT'S COLORADO HUNT
To Jack Weil
With best wishes
Ronald Reagan

CHRIS ISAAK

Man, do we have some Chris Isaak stories.

We first met Isaak when he wandered into the store before one of his Denver concerts, in 2010. We corresponded afterward, and I thanked him for inviting us to his concert at the Arvada Center.

He later wrote:

Hello Steve,

Thanks for the kind words. I'm so glad that you were able to make the show, and that you had a good experience. I could see you and Wendy right up there in front, and I was about to have you come up and do a few songs but I wasn't sure what key you do "Wild Thang" in. There is always next time right?! I had a wonderful time poking around the store, and I really appreciate your kindness and patience in showing me around. You know sometimes when you find something you really like, and then the people making it turn out to be the real deal as well . . . well I guess that just makes it even BETTER. I sincerely hope you carry on in your family tradition so that when you are about 108 I can shuffle in and pick up the newest flashy shirt. I'm loving the new shirts and belt (Thanks again!). I hope we cross paths again, and if you and Wendy find yourself out in SF please give me a holler so I can show you the great hamburger joint down the street from me!

All the best, your singing pal, Chris

OPPOSITE: Chris Isaak's autographed electric guitar is displayed in Rockmount's flagship store. More than just signed, it's an artwork.

RIGHT: Chris Isaak visits the store.

Isaak has since visited us countless times. We have seen his amazing and fully energized performances at many venues because he always invites us when he's in town.

The most recent was his holiday concert at the Paramount Theater in 2023. He really worked the crowd, strolling up every aisle and even the mezzanine to give everyone a personal experience. He deeply cares that the audience gets a good value with a memorable experience.

Another time, during an outdoor performance at the Denver Botanic Gardens a rain deluge hit. The audience stayed under umbrellas and other types of cover. While most musicians would bolt, Isaak kept playing while the crew put tarps over the electronic equipment. Then an amp blew. Did this deter him? No, he waited for a new amp and finished the concert!

My favorite story, however, is the time Isaak visited in 2013. We had lunch and I mentioned I was renovating our historic 1911 family home. He said he loved renovating and wanted to see it, so we stopped by. On the way out the front door we ran into former President Bill Clinton coming down the steps of the house across the street from us after visiting the home of Mike Fries, CEO of Liberty Global. I guess they knew each other. Bill said, "Hi, Chris," and Chris replied, "Hi, Bill." We all had a good laugh in the street and on we went.

ABOVE & BELOW : Isaak is all about the aesthetics. His mirrored concert suit is one of a kind.

TOP RIGHT: A 2011 photo with Isaak, who played with Otis Taylor (see page 124) and Anne Harris.

CHARLEY CROCKETT

Charley Crockett and Taylor Day Grace, his wife, visited Rockmount before playing Denver's Mission Ballroom in a two-night run. They bought several shirts. Charley's range is diverse: blues, country, and Americana—kinda like Rockmount? He has released sixteen albums—not bad for a self-taught guitar player. He has a full touring schedule and just keeps rising.

It is especially validating when creative people like what we do at Rockmount—same as us liking what they do!

Charley Crockett and his wife Taylor Day Grace at the store before his Mission Ballroom concert in January 2024.

ERIC STONESTREET

Actor Eric Stonestreet has visited us at Rockmount a few times since 2010 on his drive between Hollywood and his family in Kansas. He is best known for his role in *Modern Family*, for which he received two Emmys.

Eric Stonestreet sent us this photo in our signature hombre plaid No. 620.

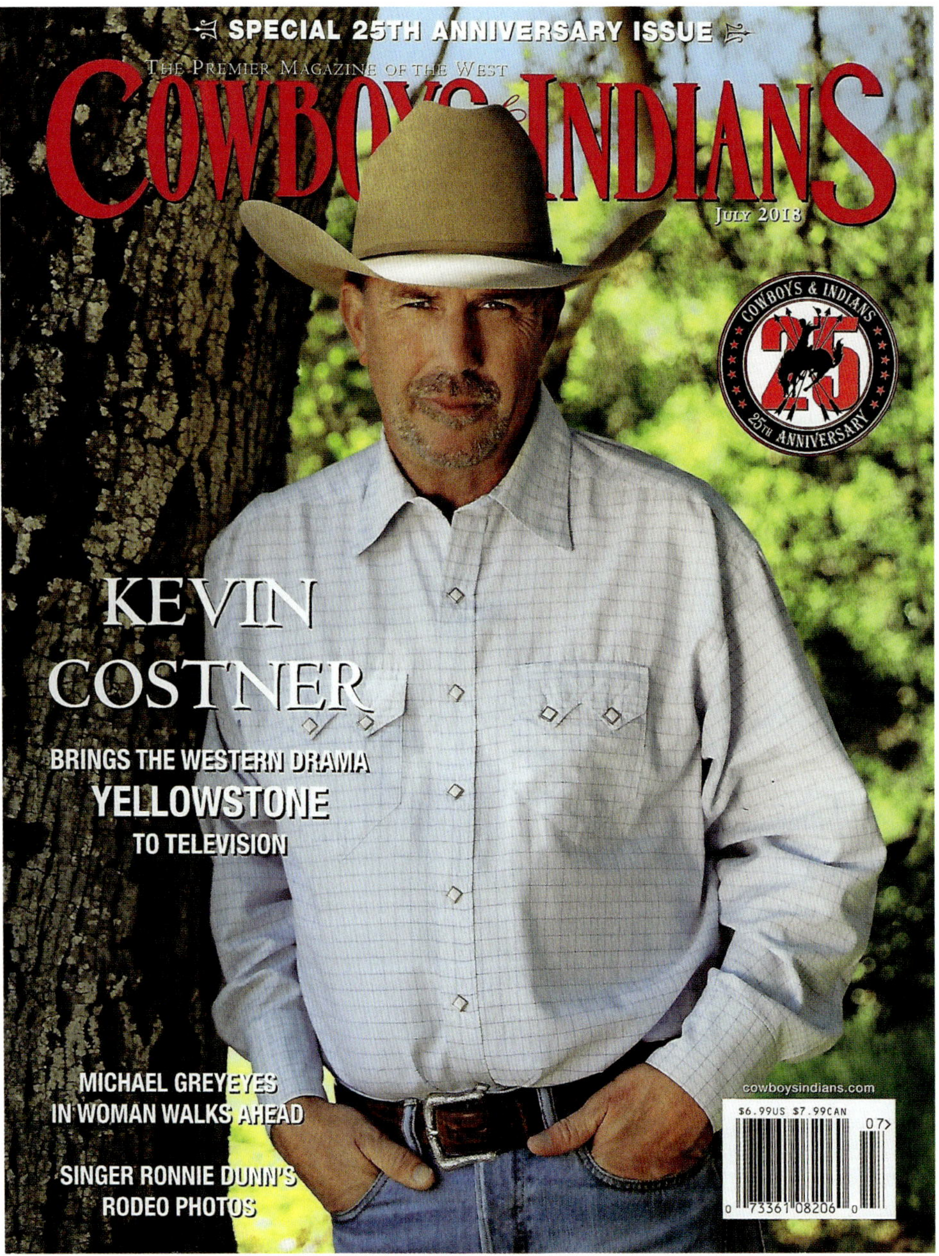

Kevin Costner in Rockmount on the cover of *Cowboys & Indians*. The issue has a feature on Paramount's television hit series *Yellowstone*. Photo courtesy *Cowboys & Indians*.

KEVIN COSTNER, *YELLOWSTONE*

Rockmount was asked to supply shirts for both male and female characters who appeared in various seasons in the Western drama series *Yellowstone*. Kevin Costner wore a tattersall check on the cover of *Cowboys & Indians*, July 2018, to commemorate the show. We also supplied shirts worn by other characters, and the series showed our banners in a rodeo scene.

James Garner. Photo courtesy *Cowboys & Indians*.

JAMES GARNER

James Garner wore Rockmount on another cover of *Cowboys & Indians* in July 2004, wearing our signature shirt design with sawtooth pockets and diamond snaps.

Daryl Hall
John Oates
Home for Christmas
Daryl Hall
John Oates

HALL & OATES

The rock duo Daryl Hall and John Oates visited Rockmount, picked up some shirts and asked us to collaborate on a custom design in 2006. It was a special, limited-edition Rockmount shirt timed with their *Home for Christmas* album release, which included a CD. The other photo is with Oates in a brown Rockmount shirt with leather applique.

OPPOSITE: This limited-edition custom design was made for the release of the Hall & Oates *Home for Christmas* album.

LEFT: Hall, wearing a Rockmount T-shirt with Wendy, Colter, and Steve Weil.

ABOVE: Oates in a brown Rockmount shirt with leather applique.

WILLIE NELSON

When pot was legalized in Colorado in 2014, the first state to do so, we made an embroidered shirt to mark the occasion, more for fun than a political statement.

Willie and his wife Annie D'Angelo sent us this photo with his new shirt No. 6712. We have also seen photos of Nelson wearing Rockmount's shadow plaids No. 693.

Esquire magazine wrote Feb. 5, 2015:

> *If you're a marijuana enthusiast (and we know some of you are judging by the response to this story), perhaps you've always wanted to wear your devotion on your sleeve, but haven't been impressed with the, um, quality of the weed-themed clothes on the market.*
>
> *Well, that's no longer a problem, thanks to venerable western shirt maker Rockmount.*
>
> *The Denver-based heritage brand that invented the snap-front western shirt recently turned its craftsman's eye to Colorado's most famous cash crop (hint, it's weed), creating an elegant, weed-adorned western shirt that recalls Gram Parsons' famous Nudie suit.*

Willie Nelson and his wife Annie D'Angelo sent us this photo with his new shirt No. 6712.

TIM MCGRAW

Country singer and actor Tim McGraw wears a trademark black straw hat. He asked Rockmount to make over 1,000 hats, which they sold on tour in 2019. We have seen photos of him wearing our denim sawtooth shirts, too.

CHRIS ROBINSON, THE BLACK CROWES

Chris Robinson, founder and lead singer of The Black Crowes, visited Rockmount while in Denver playing at Red Rocks. They come here a lot and have played many venues in town and in the mountains.

NATHANIEL RATELIFF & THE NIGHT SWEATS

We never know who is going to amble into Rockmount, but our local friend Nathaniel Rateliff shows up frequently. He performs around the world with his band The Night Sweats—Colorado boys done good. We have attended so many of the band's concerts I've lost count. The first was in 2015 at Red Rocks, and we've gone there every summer since to enjoy their concerts. Additionally, we have seen him at Denver's Mission Ballroom and even with the Colorado Symphony Orchestra. The show that I recall most fondly was when they played for a few friends on the lawn of the Colorado Governor's Mansion in 2015.

Rateliff asked us to produce a special shirt for his Marigold Foundation (above). This was a numbered, limited edition.

This photo was taken when Nathaniel Rateliff and the Night Sweats performed for a small party at the Colorado governor's mansion. Governor John Hickenlooper (now US Senator) in blue Rockmount shirt, Nathaniel Rateliff, and Steve Weil in Rockmount red shadow plaid No. 621.

AVETT BROTHERS COLLECTION

The Avett Brothers band has visited us a number of times. The first time was 2012 and they invited us to their Red Rocks concert.

Later, in 2015, we collaborated on shirts for men and women. Each shirt is a special numbered, limited edition.

Paul, Seth, me, Scott, and Joe.

The Avett Brothers
THE
Avett
BROTHERS

ALT-J

English rockers Alt-J stopped by Rockmount before their 2022 Denver Show and picked up shirts, hats, bolos, and more. While they were visiting the store, we chatted with members of the band Gus Unger-Hamilton and Joe Newman, and they invited us to the show. I mentioned my degree from the University of Bristol, England, and it turns out Unger's mom had studied there too. Now they are based in London.

It gets better. Rockmount was onstage front and center during the concert when Gus Unger-Hamilton wore Rockmount's hops design No. 6799-BEER; Joe Newman is in the Hawaiian Paniolo Hibiscus embroidery No. 6706 (below). You could feel the pulsating lighting and sound. There's nothing like good music, amazing lighting, and Rockmount onstage! A good night.

Wow, whose shirts are the band wearing?

—The band wears Rockmount.

They asked us to do a collaboration of custom shirts, which was launched during their next visit to Denver in 2023. Ahead of the concert, band members Joe Newman, Gus Unger-Hamilton, and Thom Green brought the crew for a launch party at Rockmount. Two-year-old Albin Unger was fascinated with our deer and moose heads on the wall. It brought back fond memories from my childhood when Papa Jack told us the rest of the deer was on the other side of the wall, and we kids trooped over to the company next door looking for it. . . . Anyway, it was nice hanging out with them, and they invited us to their concert—and I mean all of us—at Rockmount!

Gus Unger-Hamilton in Rockmount's Hopps shirt No. 6799-Beer, and Joe Newman in paniolo embroidery No. 6706. They wore these shirts in their concert that night. Steve (center) is in flannel plaid No. 647.

OPPOSITE: Alt-J in concert, and their special edition shirts.

FRESH OFF THE BOAT WITH RANDALL PARK

Rockmount pops up in TV shows and films frequently. The comedy show *Fresh off the Boat* with Randall Park and Constance Wu features Rockmount shirts and ties worn by Park and other characters on many episodes. We have seen at least eighteen scenes featuring Rockmount silk ties, including Nos. 409, 448, 458, 467 (2 colors), 403 (two actors), and shirts No. 609 stripe.

BARBIE MOVIE

Barbie and Ken are about as mainstream as it gets. What we have here is a meeting of the minds. Fringe has a long history, of course, with roots in Native American and mountain man culture. We have been making our popular fringe shirts No. 6723 longer than anyone else, and they got a shout-out from the movie. Additionally, Ken's buds also wore other Rockmount vintage embroideries, including styles No. 6842 and two-tone No. 6869.

Shirts worn by Ken and his buds in *Barbie.*

THE PRETENDERS

The Pretenders have visited Rockmount so many times over the years that it's hard to choose which photos to include. In fact, I went through the photos to figure out when we first met them; it was in 2009, and most recently in 2024. They have kindly invited us to all their Denver concerts.

ABOVE: Pretenders Sean Reed (keys), Nick Wilkinson (bass), Gretchen Bunn, Kristoffer Sonne (drums), Waz and me.

TOP RIGHT: Pretenders' Eric Heywood in No. 620.

BOTTOM RIGHT: Nick Wilkinson (bassist) and James Walbourne (lead guitarist) wear our bolero jacket No. 1100. Eric Heywood (pedal steel guitarist) wears our signature shadow plaid No. 620.

WORLD LEADERS ATTEND DENVER SUMMIT OF THE EIGHT + LYLE LOVETT

In 1997, world leaders from the top eight industrialized nations held a summit in Denver. It was attended by then President Bill Clinton and the heads of state from Canada, France, Germany, Italy, Japan, Russia, the United Kingdom, and the European Union. Rockmount was asked to provide the leaders with Western hats, and we were also invited to attend various events.

A highlight was an invitation to a private party where singer/songwriter Lyle Lovett also performed. Lovett has worn Rockmount shirts for many years; in the day, he bought them from Stelzigs, a Houston store that closed in 1980 after 110 years in business.

TRAILER PARK BOYS

Okay, how about some Canadian culture? It's not every day that the head of a major museum tells us he saw Rockmount worn on a television show. My favorite part of this story is how I found out about it. Ironically, our friend George Sparks—the CEO of Denver's Museum of Nature and Science, a US Air Force Academy graduate, and a tech expert—enjoys what he calls "pure mindless entertainment and anthropology, including Canada's version of *The Beverly Hillbillies.*" George told us that Bubbles, one of the main characters, wears the Rockmount No. 6726 space cowboy two-tone. He raises cats and lives in a trailer. The drunk character's ex-wife owns the trailer park.

DAVID BYRNE

If that isn't enough, David Byrne, who cofounded the new wave band Talking Heads, wore the same shirt model as Bubbles. He was seen with the Talking Heads at Red Rocks in 2018 in the red version. He also wears our orange hat No. 2453. So, how crazy that this shirt appeals to such a wide range of people, the quirkier the better? The photo came to us from a fan.

JOHN FOGERTY

John Fogerty has visited Rockmount and picked up shirts a number of times. We have seen him onstage in our No. 693 signature shadow plaid and others.

LUCINDA WILLIAMS BAND

This was published in the *Rocky Mountain News* "On the Town" column By Penny Parker, November 15, 2003:

> *BOYS (AND THEIR LEADING LADY) IN THE BAND: Lucinda Williams band members lassoed a corral's worth of shirts, boots, belts and T-shirts from Rockmount Ranch Wear in LoDo before the concert.*
>
> *"I knew them from when they worked for Dwight Yoakum, and they have stayed in touch whenever they come to Denver," said Steve Weil, Rockmount's third generation Western wear wrangler.*

The photo is especially nice because Papa Jack (center) and Jack B. (far right) are with the Lucinda Williams band in front of Rockmount.

JEMAINE CLEMENT & BRET MCKENZIE OF FLIGHT OF THE CONCHORDS

Jemaine Clement and Bret McKenzie are actors, musicians, comedians, and singers from New Zealand, and they're well known around the world. In addition to being members of the Grammy Award–winning comedy duo Flight of the Conchords, they have released several albums and created comedy series for the BBC and HBO. They have visited Rockmount a few times when in town to play Red Rocks, inviting us to their concert both times they performed at that outdoor venue. One time we sat with Bret's dad in "the good seats."

Jemaine Clement wears Rockmount two-tone steer embroidery shirt, I am in the Cream Reunion T-shirt, and Bret McKenzie has a Hawaiian floral shirt

ABOVE: Jemaine Clement wears Hall and Oates shirt.

LEFT: On a visit with me, Flight of the Conchords' Jemaine Clement is wearing Rockmount's eagle embroidery No. 6729-BLK and Bret McKenzie is in a two-tone.

OLD CROW MEDICINE SHOW

The band often visits Rockmount when playing Red Rocks. Everyone onstage wears Rockmount. One favorite memory at Red Rocks was in 2015 when they asked our friend US Senator John Hickenlooper onstage to play banjo.

ABOVE: Ketch Secor and Morgan Jahnig in Rockmount denim embroideries.

RIGHT: Chance McCoy in Rockmount chambray No. 640-C and Steve Weil in red plaid during a visit to the store.

OPPOSITE: Old Crow Medicine Show band in concert at Red Rocks, all in Rockmount.

COLLABORATIONS

In the same way that Rockmount has been a longtime favorite of rock stars and movie makers, we have collaborated with many major leading brands and organizations over the years to produce branded merchandise. It is an honor to be associated with them, and we believe it has created lasting goodwill.

Along the way, we have also been asked to create shirts, hats, and accessories for an amazing array of public and private organizations, from the United States Congress to museums, national parks, universities, rodeos, hotels, theme parks, and even the occasional motorcycle "club." (More about that strange story later.)

HONORS

The year 2008 was a significant one in Rockmount's history, for reasons both poignant and professional. It was the year we lost both my father and later my grandfather. Yet I am reminded of my grandfather's query to me early in 2008 about our plans for the Democratic National Convention to be held in Denver that August and where US Senator Barack Obama was the nominee. The *New York Times* published two articles about Rockmount in relation to the convention. The first one, on January 12, 2007, was a scoop saying we knew Denver was selected over New York City before it was public:

> *At least one business owner here said he had known that the convention was coming. How?*
>
> *Because of a shirt.*
>
> *Steven Weil, who owns Rockmount Ranch Wear in downtown Denver—shirts with snaps, dudes in chaps—said someone in the "inner circle" of the selection process, whom he declined to identify, called several weeks ago to place an order. Denver, Mr. Weil decided then, was in.*

Later, on August 8, 2008, the *New York Times* ran a feature story about what to do in Denver during the convention.

How the West Was Worn

New York Times, August 8, 2008

Let's say you have an image problem. Some people, misguided as they may be, think you are an elitist. Now, that's nothing that can't be fixed with a little fashion makeover at Rockmount Ranch Wear (1626 Wazee Street; 303-629-7777; www.rockmount.com), a LoDo shop famous in these parts for introducing the snap button to the western shirt, making it easier for cowboys to ride the range or re-enact scenes from "Brokeback Mountain." (Yep, Jack and Ennis were Rockmount customers.)

The store and an accompanying museum have the fascinating feel of history, with a lasso-rope logo and vintage displays, but the shirts have modern-day prices, most of them $62 to $84. Steve Weil, the president of Rockmount, is creating a special style for the convention, based on Denver's abstract mountain flag, designed for the United States Congressional Delegation.

DENVER • SATURDAY, AUGUST 25, 2007 • $1.00

Rocky Mountai

COUNTDOWN TO DENVER

Oh, say can you DNC?

Dress them, feed them, house them, get them wired and wireless, schmooze them and don't forget all those welcoming parties – those are among the jobs of this quintet charged with getting the Mile High City ready for the Democratic National Convention one year away.

The lineup, from left to right:

- **Steve Weil, president of Rockmount Ranch Wear** Job: Make the conventioneers look and feel Western (make that snaps, not buttons), at least temporarily.
- **Brook Colangelo, DNC director of technology** Job: Create a technology web to connect the convention with the rest of the world. Have a "green" plan for the aftermath.
- **Elbra Wedgeworth, host committee president** Job: Convince 10,000 people to volunteer for four very intense days, preferably 10,000 smiling people.
- **Steve Farber, host committee co-chairman** Job: Help potential donors understand that it takes money, as in *their* money, to stage a convention.
- **Larry DiPasquale, president Epicurean Catering** Job: Think dinner party, a very large dinner party.

NEWS 20

The front page of the daily *Rocky Mountain News* also featured our company as one reason, among many, that Denver was selected for the convention.

So, when Papa (a lifelong Republican) asked what we had planned for the DNC, I told him we had designed a shirt for over 400 congressional delegates who would be attending.

Serendipity played a big part. Long-time Colorado Congresswoman Diana DeGette had already asked me to create a shirt reflecting both Denver and Colorado. As luck would have it, I'd already worked on one that my friend Mayor John Hickenlooper (later governor, and now US senator) had asked me to design for the city but later was unsure where to use it. So, that Rockmount shirt was picked by the congressional delegation to wear for the four-day event awash with famous people from across the US and abroad. We were invited to many events.

In fact, since 1980, Rockmount has been asked by both of Colorado's major political parties to supply Western shirts and straw hats for both Democratic and Republican US presidential conventions. Rockmount has done its best to give each its own Colorado identity.

My father, Jack B., had served as a moderate leader in the Colorado Republican Party for many years and was a delegate to every RNC convention from 1980 to 2004.

LEFT: This Rockmount flag motif straw hat has been popular at the conventions of both parties.

ABOVE: Michele Obama's grandmother, Delores Robinson, visiting Rockmount in her official DNC shirt.

PURPLE HEART

Rockmount was asked to create a special shirt for the Purple Heart honorees for their national event held in Denver, 2014. This black cotton gabardine twill shirt has the medal embroidered on the collar and lavender flowers tracing the shirt's yokes.

MEDAL OF HONOR

Just after the Democratic National Convention, Denver hosted the annual convention of the Congressional Medal of Honor Society, which brings together the nation's most honored military heroes. Longtime Denver-based billionaire philanthropist Phil Anschutz and his family underwrote the event. Rockmount was privileged to create the shirt for 150 Medal of Honor recipients. The design is an elegant, solid black cotton gabardine twill snap shirt with the medal's official blue stars insignia embroidery and matching piping and snaps.

Its embroidered motto: VALOR * COURAGE * HONOR.

The hosts invited me to attend the gala, where I met actor/film director Clint Eastwood, who was also honored during the event.

MUSEUMS

Since the 1990s, Rockmount has developed close working relationships with several major museums around the country.

As a lifelong museophile, having personally visited hundreds of museums across the world, I have been honored to be asked to collaborate with museums on their Western fashion exhibits and merchandise. To Rockmount, there is no higher standard or validation than "museum quality."

SMITHSONIAN

The Smithsonian, the world's largest museum, education and research complex, was the first museum to come calling.

It was the early 1990s, and the Washington, DC, institution asked us for shirts and memorabilia for their collection. Since then, Rockmount has worked with several museums that have hosted exhibits featuring our brand. We've also collaborated with museums to reproduce historic designs, but also new shirts and scarves to be sold in museum stores.

DENVER ART MUSEUM

The Denver Art Museum has featured Rockmount in numerous fashion exhibits and carries the brand in its store. Rockmount produced bandanas for the museum. A 1950s fashion exhibit in 2018 included a black Rockmount shirt and bolo.

THE NATIONAL COWGIRL MUSEUM & HALL OF FAME

Not limited to cowboys, Rockmount has enjoyed working with the National Cowgirl Museum for many years. At right is a scarf they asked us to make in 2022.

BUFFALO BILL CENTER OF THE WEST

In 2003, Rockmount was invited to attend the Western Design Conference in Cody, Wyoming, at the Buffalo Bill Center of the West, an affiliate of the Smithsonian. Rockmount had a display in the museum in 2003, which began a long-term relationship with them.

Our first project was to reproduce a silk scarf worn by Buffalo Bill in the nineteenth century. Through his Wild West Shows, the American frontiersman (born William Frederick Cody), showman, and entrepreneur is credited with popularizing the American West throughout the USA and the world.

We also made a highly stylized shirt for the BBCW museum store commemorating Buffalo Bill. It has design elements from Buffalo Bill's buckskin outfit.

TOP: In 2009, the BBCW's Whitney Western Art Museum commissioned us to make a silk scarf commemorating its fiftieth anniversary. The collection is named for its patron Gertrude Vanderbilt Whitney. The scarf features six important paintings.

BOTTOM: A Rockmount exhibit at the Buffalo Bill Center of the West.

OPPOSITE, TOP LEFT: Buffalo Bill wore the original of this scarf from the museum's collection. The floral and bird design silk scarf No. BB-BUFF is a numbered, limited edition and remains popular, available at the museum store and at Rockmount.

OPPOSITE, TOP RIGHT: In 2025, the museum requested we create another silk scarf. This numbered, limited edition is a contemporary design. It can be worn or displayed as a collectible work of art.

OPPOSITE, BOTTOM LEFT AND RIGHT: This shirt was a collaboration with the museum based on the buckskin shirt in the museum collection. It features special scallop embroidery on the front center and floral embroidery based on the original.

Buffalo Bill's
Wild West Show

AUTRY MUSEUM OF THE AMERICAN WEST AND NATIONAL COWBOY & WESTERN HERITAGE CENTER

While researching for my *Western Shirts* book in the early 2000s, I worked with several museums and reviewed their archives of vintage Western wear, including Rockmount. Among them were the Autry Museum of the American West in Los Angeles and the National Cowboy & Western Heritage Museum in Oklahoma City.

The Autry Museum plays into Rockmount's story in a myriad of ways. The curator asked us to reproduce a number of shirts, including styles associated with the prominent country singer Porter Wagoner and the legendary singer and actor Gene Autry, known as "The Singing Cowboy." Rockmount's Porter Wagoner shirt remains in production today and is one of the most elaborate embroideries our company has made.

Additionally, both museums have exhibited many Rockmount items over the years, including the pivotal shirts worn in the 2005 movie *Brokeback Mountain*. In fact, the plaid Rockmount shirt worn by Heath Ledger's character in that film, along with the denim Rockmount shirt worn by Jake Gyllenhaal's character, later sold for $101,000 at a charity auction.

We have visited the National Cowboy Museum many times to attend special exhibits featuring Western fashion, including Rockmount. We have a close relationship with the NCWH and have worked with the museum and its curators on exhibits, providing clothing, accessories, and memorabilia from Rockmount. The museum has carried Rockmount designs in their shop for decades.

In 2022, the *Western Wares* exhibit featured over 10,000 square feet of Native American and Western furniture, jewelry, and fashion, including twenty-plus items from Rockmount's collection. In conjunction with the same exhibit, we collaborated with the museum on additional custom shirt and bandana designs.

Both shirts were collaborations with the Autry Museum. Above is the Porter Wagoner shirt, No. 6755, one of the most ornate designs ever made by Rockmount and still in production. The green shirt is a design worn by Gene Autry.

Colors I like

Flowers

EMBROIDERY FROM THE DRC COLLECTION

Style for Buffalo Bill

NATIONAL COWBOY & WESTERN HERITAGE ★ MUSEUM ★

Denim shirts designed for the *Western Wares* exhibit, 2014.

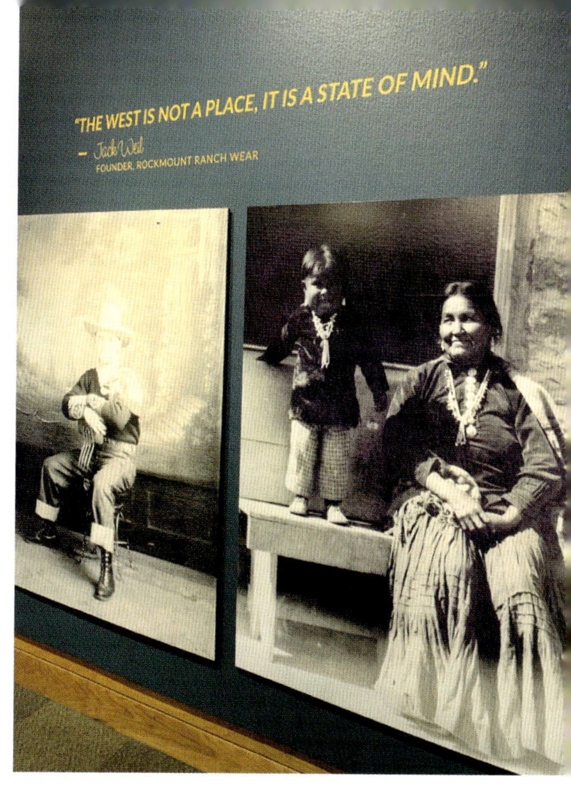

TOP: The exhibit entrance features a Jack A. Weil quotation.

BOTTOM: The National Cowboy & Western Heritage Museum asked us in 2022 to produce a special scarf celebrating their annual patrons Prix de West invitational art show.

ABOVE: The official shirt for the museum and exhibit. The shirt is based on a 1950s design by Jack B. Weil with "Quarter Horse" pockets and yokes and three-point cuffs.

BELOW: Wendy and Steve Weil with Reed Weimer at the opening of *Cowboys & Rock Stars* exhibit.

FOOTHILLS ART CENTER

In 2011, and closer to home, the Foothills Art Center in Golden, Colorado, produced a different kind of exhibit, focused exclusively on Rockmount's history. They called it *Cowboys & Rock Stars*. It included over 2,500 square feet of Rockmount clothing, accessories, hats, advertising, original catalog illustrations, and memorabilia. An entire room was devoted to rock stars such as Bob Dylan, Eric Clapton, Paul McCartney, and Jack White wearing Rockmount. Rockmount produced a commemorative shirt for the exhibit based on a 1950s Jack B. Weil embroidered columbine, Colorado's official state flower.

HISTORY COLORADO CENTER

The museum at Denver's History Colorado Center has highlighted Rockmount in several exhibits and its shop over the years. In 2017, Rockmount was in *Back Story*, an exhibit on the American West as a source of inspiration in dramatic landscapes and lifestyle. The West is seen as an alternative to urban sameness.

Surrounding the Rockmount display were major artworks by Albert Bierstadt, Ernest Martin Hennings, Thomas Moran, Allen Tupper True, Frank Mechau, and others. The juxtaposition of these iconic works with Rockmount shirts provides meaningful context on the history of the West. Many of the early American artists were European, and they took their works home, which helped to spread the romance of the West.

Currently the *Zoom In* exhibit features 100 powerful artifacts on how Colorado became Colorado and includes two 1950s Rockmount shirts designed by Jack B. Weil: a men's black horseshoe applique with saddle stitching and a women's yellow sleeveless with mirrored pockets.

ABOVE: Rockmount 1950s horseshoe applique shirts in black for men and sleeveless gold for women on long-term display at History Colorado.

BELOW: The museum's exhibit featuring fine Western art and Rockmount in its exhibit on the American West.

A.R. MITCHELL MUSEUM

The A.R. Mitchell Museum of Western Art, in Trinidad, Colorado, asked Rockmount to design a special bandana for its 2021 gala.

NORTH CAROLINA MUSEUM OF HISTORY

In 2022 the North Carolina Museum of History opened an exhibit entitled "The Power of Women in Country Music." They asked us to create a bandana for the exhibit.

LEFT: Bandana for A.R. Mitchell Museum.
RIGHT: North Carolina Museum of History bandana.

WINGS OVER THE ROCKIES

In 2023, Denver's Wings Over the Rockies Air & Space Museum asked Rockmount to create this shirt to commemorate the Boeing B-52 Stratofortress for its collection. The aircraft has been used by the United States Air Force since the 1950s. NASA has also used this aircraft for over fifty years.

MUSEUM OF CONTEMPORARY ART

The Museum of Contemporary Art, Denver, asked Rockmount to create a special bandana for its 2024 *Cowboy* exhibit.

DENVER INTERNATIONAL AIRPORT

Denver International Airport holds exhibits on the concourse; they featured Rockmount in 2011 and 2017. As one of the busiest airports in the world, over sixty million passengers passed through it in 2017. The exhibit showcased Rockmount, celebrities who wear its shirts, and memorabilia.

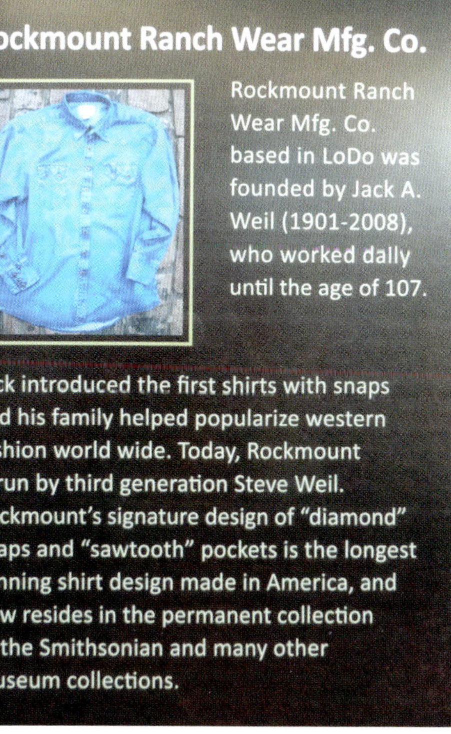

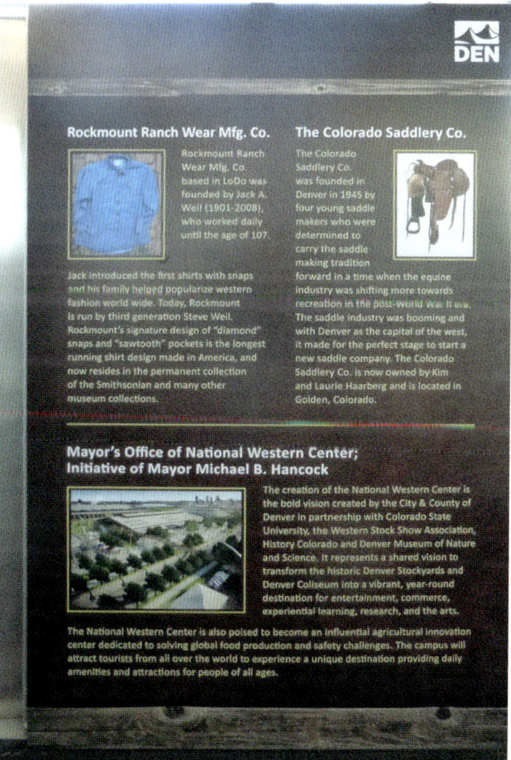

Also featured is the shirt made for Colorado State University and worn by Temple Grandin, renowned professor of Animal Science.

RODEOS AND STATE FAIRS

Rodeos and stock shows have branded Western merchandise every year for more than a hundred years, since the advent of rodeos. You see trophy saddles, buckles, shirts, ties, and scarves branded by the many rodeos. Rockmount has been selected by many to do projects over the years. All of these designs are collaborations that they asked us to make.

Rockmount has enjoyed a longtime partnership with Denver's National Western Stock Show. Over the years, the event's organizers have asked us to produce a wide range of items, including a tie celebrating the stock show's Centennial Anniversary in 2006. We collaborated with our friend, fine artist Duke Beardsley, to create a commemorative silk tie.

In 2018 to commemorate the recent massive expansion of the National Western facilities, we were asked to create a medallion. It is based on one from 1909 in our collection. A new silk tie and scarf commemorate the 120th anniversary (2026), based on the art of Kathryn Merrill.

LEFT: National Western Stock Show 100th Anniversary silk tie with tag.

ABOVE: National Western medallion we created in 2018 to commemorate the $1 billion expansion of the National Western Stock Show facilities.

RIGHT: Silk scarf and tie created to commemorate the 120th anniversary of the National Western Stock Show

LEFT: We created this special pin to commemorate the Rustlers' 40th Anniversary, 2024.

BELOW, TOP: Wearing the Rustlers shirt: is US Senator Michael Bennet (left), who said, "Rockmount is the best shirt I have."

BELOW, BOTTOM:: State Representative Sean Camacho, Steve Weil, and Governor Jared Polis.

DENVER RUSTLERS SUPPORT 4-H AT COLORADO STATE FAIR

Since 1984, the Denver Rustlers have been fundraising for Colorado's 4-H youth who compete at the annual Colorado State Fair in Pueblo. The Rustlers group of three hundred Colorado business and professional and government leaders support kids who raise, show, and sell their livestock at the fair's auction. The Rustlers all wear a Rockmount straw hat and a custom vintage embroidered shirt. The shirt is based on an original art deco design created in the 1950s by Jack B. Weil. The Rustlers fund over $250,000 in auction sales annually, which not only supports the state's agricultural heritage but helps send the kids to college.

HOUSTON & FORT WORTH STOCK SHOWS, CHEYENNE FRONTIER DAYS, CALGARY STAMPEDE

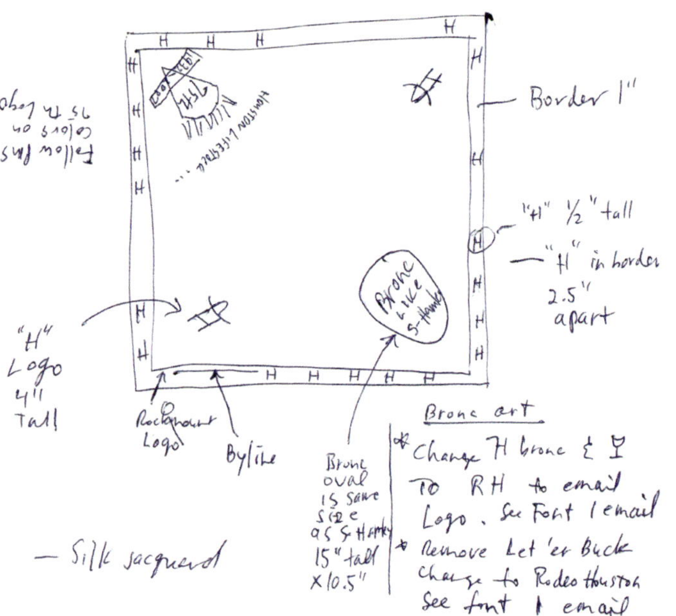

The Cheyenne Frontier Days, aka "The Daddy of 'em All," has asked us to produce many products over the years, including leather inlaid bronc bomber jackets, shirts, silk ties, and scarves. The silk tie is a design from our collection with Cheyenne Frontier Days' logo added. The bomber jacket, above, is in the CFD Old West Museum.

In 2007, the Houston Livestock Show and Rodeo commissioned this limited-edition silk scarf. The design sketch is above.

LEFT AND ABOVE: Silk ties and a scarf made for the Calgary Stampede.

Similarly, Rockmount has worked with the Calgary Stampede on many products over the years—buckles, shirts, silk scarves, and ties. We create new artwork and also add their logo to our designs.

We made silk ties and scarves at the request of the Fort Worth Rodeo & Stock Show.

The American Royal in Kansas City asked us to make shirts with this embroidery.

RANCHES & SADDLE CLUBS

Over the decades, Rockmount has created hundreds, if not thousands, of custom shirts for ranches and saddle clubs. The earliest of these I have come across was our signature No. 6801 highly stylized 1950s white "Quarter Horse" design with raglan sleeves, saddle stitching, single point cuffs and embroidered with the name "Kualoa Ranch." That ranch, founded in 1850 on the island of Oahu, is one of the oldest operating cattle ranches in the United States. You can imagine how thrilled I was to discover one of the shirts in 2002 at a Honolulu vintage clothing store called Island Treasures Antique Mall.

Over many years, we have added riding club embroidery to our staple designs. Our No. 640 shirt with sawtooth pockets and diamond snaps is the longest-running shirt design in America. It was used for countless custom orders, including the Lazy K and White Lake saddle clubs. These club shirts are typical of those made in the US since the 1950s.

Rockmount continues to work with saddle clubs near and far. One riding club is the Los Caballeros. Since 1949, it has dedicated itself to preserving the Western heritage and cowboy culture on Catalina Island, off the Southern California coast. They have been ordering their official shirts from us for many years.

Examples of ranch and saddle club shirts made in the 1950s. The white Kualoa Ranch has all kinds of special treatments. The red Silver Riders Ass'n shirt is notable for its extra embellishment, with rhinestone stars on the collar, pocket flaps, and lining yokes and pockets. Heavy special treatments like this, made in the USA, were prevalent during the so-called Golden Age of Western Wear, from the 1940s-60s, but gave way as US labor costs soared in the 1960s. The red, turquoise, and black shirts are more recent remakes.

ABOVE RIGHT: In Southern California, the Santa Monica Police Department's Mounted Patrol has ordered its custom shirts.

BELOW RIGHT: In 2025, the Main Street Cowboys, a group of volunteers who work at the annual Pendleton Round-Up rodeo in Oregon, asked us to remake this style of two-tone shirt, which the group has worn for decades.

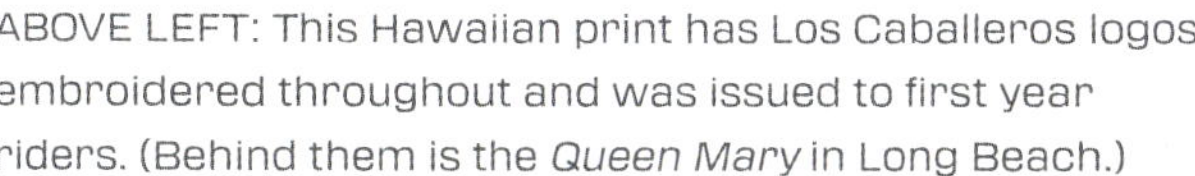
ABOVE LEFT: This Hawaiian print has Los Caballeros logos embroidered throughout and was issued to first year riders. (Behind them is the *Queen Mary* in Long Beach.)

BELOW LEFT: The club invited me to ride with them in recent years, and we have produced various shirts, including this navy stars design.

BEER & SPIRITS

Rockmount has teamed up with dozens of major alcohol beverage companies including Coors, Shiner, Stranahan's, and Jack Daniels among others. We have created branded products for these companies, ranging from belts and hats to shirts.

When Jack Daniel's heard my grandfather, Papa Jack, on national news say that he attributed his longevity to drinking their whiskey, they ran some promotional media, including his image. They also sent him a special vintage whiskey each year for his birthday. It came with a letter from the master distiller.

HOTELS, THEME PARKS, VENUES AND CLUBS

THE BROADMOOR HOTEL

A funny thing happened on the way to the . . . actually, it was at an event in 2018 for the Colorado Music Hall of Fame at the Denver Convention Center. I was standing at the bar and the man next to me said, "Tell me about your tie." I was stunned. How many billionaires do you run into? It was Phil Anschutz, who, among his diverse holdings, has the finest collection of Western Art in the world, mostly displayed in the American Museum of Western Art. I said I had long wanted to collaborate with him on our silk collection. He asked me for my card.

The very next morning, he called and asked if I could stop by his office. I did, and even his office walls are filled with an unequaled art collection. We made a plan to produce a series of limited-edition buckles, ties, and scarves based on the art. We created a silk scarf and buckle based on the Maxfield Parish painting *The Broadmoor Hotel*.

The Broadmoor Resort in Colorado Springs asked us to make silk ties, scarves, and buckles based on the Maxfield Parrish painting. We also work with their Anschutz Collection on custom products for the American Museum of Western Art, the largest private collection of Western art in the country.

We based our design for this silk tie and scarf combination on the early American painting *Long Jakes, Rocky Mountain Man*, by Charles Deas, courtesy of the Denver Art Museum and the American Museum of Western Art—The Anschutz Collection, which share joint ownership.

This tie and scarf collection is based on the early American painting *The Lost Greenhorn*, by Alfred Jacob Miller, courtesy of the American Museum of Western Art—The Anschutz Collection.

LEFT: The Yellowstone Club, Big Sky, Montana, carries Rockmount in its store and commissioned us to make this branded silk scarf based on our signature bronc.

BELOW: The historic Gage Hotel in Marathon, Texas, known for its White Buffalo Bar, orders Rockmount for its store and staff uniforms.

Ronnie Dunn's No. 6666 black leather shirt on display in the Country Music Hall of Fame.

NASHVILLE & THE COUNTRY MUSIC HALL OF FAME

Nashville has always been a major market for Rockmount, so it's no surprise that we work with the legendary Country Music Hall of Fame. They display Ronnie Dunn's Rockmount black leather shirt No. 6666, which he wore onstage and in music videos. The shop has a Rockmount department.

The Grand Ole Opry and Ryman Auditorium asked us to create a shirt and buckle collection.

DODGE MOTOR COMPANY, SEAWORLD, CASA BONITA

Rockmount has designed items for other well-known brands, including ties and shirts for Dodge Motor Company, wardrobe pieces for performers at SeaWorld, custom bandanas for the Visit Denver tourist bureau, and a buckle for the Fort Worth Stockyards.

Even Casa Bonita, the iconic Mexican restaurant/diving show in Lakewood, Colorado, which is now owned by the creators of *South Park*, asked us to design a full range of wardrobe for the cast to wear in Western vignettes when not cliff diving, including this shirt.

SeaWorld asked us to make their wardrobe shirts and skirts for performers in a Western theme production.

Shirt for Casa Bonita.

For Dodge Motor Company, we made shirts and silk ties.

MOTORCYCLE CLUBS

The Antique Motorcycle Club commissioned us to make these shirts. This shows the wide-ranging interest in Western wear beyond traditional markets.

UNDEAD RIDERS 666 POSSE

Sometimes custom projects do not turn out as expected.

In 2004, in one of my earliest custom projects, Rockmount was asked to make custom shirts for a motorcycle "club" called Undead Riders 666 Posse.

They paid a deposit, took delivery of the shirts, and all went well—until they ordered another run of the custom shirts. But this time, against my better judgment, Rockmount did not ask for a deposit.

The shirts were finished and ready for payment, but for some reason, despite repeated attempts, we could not reach the buyer. Finally, someone responded that the buyer was doing ten to twenty.

So, there we were, stuck with these shirts. What was I to do?

We rolled the dice and decided to sell them online—along with the story. Wouldn't you know, the shirts sold out so quickly to the public that we continued to run the design for a while. People liked them.

I had also learned an important lesson: stick to the deposit requirement on custom orders!

Modeled by a Rockmount employee.

HIGHER EDUCATION

Rockmount was asked to design branded shirts for the University of Colorado featuring the school's colors of black and gold, accented with a floral embroidery.

Colorado State University is another Rockmount customer, ordering special green shirts with a yellow floral and logo embroidery.

Turns out, CSU has one of our greatest ambassadors in Dr. Temple Grandin, a professor of Animal Science, and world-renowned spokesperson on autism, as well as humane livestock handling.

Dr. Grandin (see page 167) is often photographed wearing Rockmount shirts. We couldn't be more flattered.

LEFT: Official shirt of Colorado State University with the Rams logo.

ABOVE: Official shirt of University of Colorado for regents and leadership. Note the CU logo incorporated in the back embroidery.

Photograph Credits

T=top, M=middle, B=bottom, L=left, R=right

Barack Obama Presidential Library, The, National Archives, 96 B
Billy Martin's, New York, 44 TR, 96 T
Billy Strings, 120
Brian Setzer Orchestra, 105
Eric Clapton, 44 TL, 52
Tim Collins, 185
Cowboys & Indians, 132, 133
Elvis Presley Enterprises & Graceland, 44 BR, 49
Esquire, 73
Focus Features, 44 MR and Row 3 L, 72, 73 T
GQ, 92
Longmire/Garson Studios, 107 R
NBC Universal, 44 MR, 44 Row 3 L
Povy Kendal Atchison, 37
Propaganda Films & Polygram Film Entertainment, 44 ML, 63
Paramount Pictures, 109
David Parker, painting, 20, end sheets
Scott Pelley and CBS *60 Minutes*, 70
Rocky Mountain News, 124, 155 R
Ronald Reagan Presidential Library, The, 44 MM, 58, 59, 60, 61
Eric Stonestreet, 131 B
Universal Pictures, 106 T
Warner Bros., 44 BL, 62
Steve Weil & Rockmount Ranch Wear Mfg. Co., © 2026, 6, 7, 8, 10, 11, 12, 13, 14, 15, 16, 19, 20, 21 T&B, 23, 24, 25, 26, 27, 28, 29, 30, 33, 34, 36, 38, 40, 41, 42, 43, 44 TM, 44 BM, 45, 46, 47, 48, 50, 53, 56, 57, 58 inset, 63 B, 64, 65, 66, 67, 68, 69, 74, 76, 77, 78, 79, 80, 81, 82, 84, 85, 86, 88, 89, 91, 93, 94, 97, 98, 99, 100, 101, 102, 103, 106 B, 107 L, 108, 110, 111, 112, 113, 114, 116, 117, 118, 119, 120 T, 121, 122, 123, 125, 126, 127, 128, 129, 130, 131 T, 134, 135, 137, 138, 139, 140, 141, 142, 143, 146, 147, 148, 149, 150, 151, 152, 153, 154, 155 TL, 158, 159, 160, 161, 162, 163, 164, 165, 166, 177, 168, 169, 170, 171, 172, 173, 174, 175, 176, 177, 178, 179, 180, 181, 182
Western Wear & Trade Equipment, 17
Willie Nelson and Annie D'Angelo, 136

Acknowledgments

Where to start? Of course, there would be no Rockmount—no snap shirts?—no story without my grandfather's and father's lifelong careers building the company. Their foundation built its lasting role as a leader in the fashion industry. My grandmother Bea once said "the business was a mistress," but I think it's an extension of the family.

The Colorado Historical Foundation, within History Colorado, gave us a preservation grant in 2005, seed money to renovate the 1909 Rockmount Building, which helped us pivot into the future. We had just completed a family buyout of the building, so it was a crucial time to be deeply challenged by a big mortgage, as well as the collapse of the retail landscape and the dot.com recession. The grant reinforced our commitment to invest in the future. It gave us the confidence to reinvent both the use of the building and the company. This helps navigate ups and downs, including the profound impact of the COVID-19 pandemic.

I am thankful for some excellent English teachers, who gave me a foundation that I have drawn upon since becoming an author. My high school AP English teacher, Dudley Enos, influenced my passion for good reading and writing. My freshman year honors English professor at Tulane, Purvis Boyette, forcibly taught me English as a first language. Finding one's muse—a compelling subject—and the right words to tell that story is the ultimate challenge of the writer.

None of this happens in a vacuum. It started with our wholesale retail store partners spanning the country, Europe, Asia, and Canada, who supported the brand since day one. I am also grateful for the support of the public when we opened our flagship retail store in 2005, and later when we went online. The media—print, TV, film—helped put us on the radar.

The music world has been instrumental, taking the brand onstage. I love the performers' friendly visits to our store and their invitations to attend their concerts. In the same way our clothing and accessory collections are varied, so is our following, which crosses generations, urban and rural, and so many other boundaries across the spectrum.

Thank you to the many museums that exhibit Rockmount and carry the brand in their stores, giving us a special place in popular culture.

Wendy, my ever-patient wife, has supported these many paradigm shifts since we met in 1992. She immersed herself solidly in the Western lifestyle, tangential to her couture fashion modeling background. I am deeply grateful for her partnership.

The staff at Rockmount make the trains run on time—no small feat. Indeed, it's a big village. I'm also thankful for our suppliers and the factories with whom we work daily.

Every writer needs an editor. So, finally, my most heartfelt thanks to one of my oldest friends, Tracy Seipel, a former newspaper reporter and editor, who did the first edit. Sharpening words to get clearer meaning is an art form.

Thanks to Joe Daniels for his intellectual property advice.

The folks at Gibbs Smith have for decades been making good books for the soul. Gibbs himself, now gone, both inspired and enabled me to become an author with my first book. The company published *Western Shirts* in 2004, a wonderful experience. Twenty years later, editor Madge Baird pitched me for a new version. Our discussions led to a new book chronicling Rockmount's celebrity following, which has grown so much over the years. The team at Gibbs Smith had the vision, motivating me to do this project. I am so grateful.

Steve Weil

Western wear is in Steve Weil's genes. He is the third generation to run Rockmount Ranch Wear Mfg. Co., founded in 1946. He joined the company in 1981, taking its sales internationally to most developed countries. Since the 1980s, he has headed design and merchandising. Steve has built on the design foundation of his father and grandfather. Rockmount offers over two hundred styles of shirts for adults and children, and the signature "sawtooth" pocket and "diamond" snap design is the longest-running shirt design in America. Steve updated fit and introduced fabrics and colors not previously used in Western wear. He also introduced the Rockmount Vintage Collection, which is faithful to the Golden Age of Western design, from the 1940s–60s. Beyond that, his contribution to Western fashion has been to bring back a plethora of special treatments long since abandoned, where fabrics have to be custom made and embroidery done by hand. Under Steve's leadership, he is preserving both the family's fashion role and tradition as well as the company's headquarters. Rockmount remains in its original location, the restored 1909 Rockmount Building in lower downtown Denver's historic district, near Union Station and Coors Field.

Steve literally wrote the book on Western wear, *Western Shirts: A Classic American Fashion* (Gibbs Smith, 2004), which surveys seventy years of design and the people and companies who popularized the style. He has degrees from Tulane University (BA), University of Bristol, UK (Law), and the University of Colorado (MBA). He lives in Denver, Colorado, with his wife, Wendy, who works in the retail side of the business; their yellow Labrador, Humboldt, is chief of security. Their son, Colter, dodged the rag trade; he works in finance.

Author portrait courtesy Tim Collins.

Index

Celebrities

Honors & Collaborations